Pirate Trails

A WORLD BANK STUDY

Pirate Trails
Tracking the Illicit Financial Flows from Pirate Activities off the Horn of Africa

© 2013 International Bank for Reconstruction and Development / The World Bank
1818 H Street NW, Washington DC 20433
Telephone: 202-473-1000; Internet: www.worldbank.org

Some rights reserved

1 2 3 4 16 15 14 13

World Bank Studies are published to communicate the results of the Bank's work to the development community with the least possible delay. The manuscript of this paper therefore has not been prepared in accordance with the procedures appropriate to formally edited texts.

This work is a product of the staff of The World Bank with external contributions. Note that The World Bank does not necessarily own each component of the content included in the work. The World Bank therefore does not warrant that the use of the content contained in the work will not infringe on the rights of third parties. The risk of claims resulting from such infringement rests solely with you.

The findings, interpretations, and conclusions expressed in this work do not necessarily reflect the views of The World Bank, its Board of Executive Directors, or the governments they represent. The World Bank does not guarantee the accuracy of the data included in this work. The boundaries, colors, denominations, and other information shown on any map in this work do not imply any judgment on the part of The World Bank concerning the legal status of any territory or the endorsement or acceptance of such boundaries.

Nothing herein shall constitute or be considered to be a limitation upon or waiver of the privileges and immunities of The World Bank, all of which are specifically reserved.

Rights and Permissions

This work is available under the Creative Commons Attribution 3.0 Unported license (CC BY 3.0) **http://creativecommons.org/licenses/by/3.0.** Under the Creative Commons Attribution license, you are free to copy, distribute, transmit, and adapt this work, including for commercial purposes, under the following conditions:

Attribution—Please cite the work as follows: World Bank. 2013. *Pirate Trails: Tracking the Illicit Financial Flows from Pirate Activities off the Horn of Africa.* A World Bank Study. Washington, DC: World Bank. doi:10.1596/978-0-8213-9963-7.

Translations—If you create a translation of this work, please add the following disclaimer along with the attribution: *This translation was not created by The World Bank and should not be considered an official World Bank translation. The World Bank shall not be liable for any content or error in this translation.*

All queries on rights and licenses should be addressed to World Bank Publications, The World Bank Group, 1818 H Street NW, Washington, DC 20433, USA; fax: 202-522-2625; e-mail: pubrights@worldbank.org.

ISBN (paper): 978-0-8213-9963-7
ISBN (electronic): 978-1-4648-0041-2
DOI: 10.1596/978-0-8213-9963-7

Cover photo: iStock.com/GBlakeley. *Cover design*: Corporate Visions, Inc.

Library of Congress Cataloging-in Publication Data has been requested.

Contents

Acknowledgments — *ix*
Contributors — *xiii*
Abbreviations — *xvii*

Executive Summary — 1
    Somali Piracy: Criminal Networks — 2
    Main Recommendations — 4

Section I   **Introduction** — 7

Chapter 1   **"I Am a Pirate"** — 9
    Why This Study? — 9
    Pirate Financiers and Pirates — 10
    The Pirates Talk… — 11
    Key Terms Used in the Study — 12
    Outline of the Study — 14
    Notes — 14

Chapter 2   **The Context for This Study** — 17
    Audience — 17
    Methodological Framework — 17
    Notes — 23

Chapter 3   **Background on Piracy** — 25
    Origins of Somali Piracy — 25
    Current Situation in Somalia — 25
    Somali Piracy: A Gateway out of Poverty — 27
    Criminal Influence on the Economy — 29
    Somali Pirate Networks — 29
    The Somali Piracy Business Model — 30
    Somali Piracy: Problems and Responses — 32
    Notes — 34

Section II	**Understanding the Financial Flows**	**37**
Chapter 4	Ransoms	39
	Starting Point: Law Firms Negotiating Ransoms	39
	How Much Money Are We Talking About?	40
	Explaining the "Peak" of 2011 and the Decrease in 2012	42
	Notes	44
Chapter 5	Distributing the Proceeds	45
	Low-Level Pirates—"Foot Soldiers"	45
	Monies Flowing to Local Communities	46
	The Lions' Share: How Do Financiers Invest and Benefit from Piracy?	47
	The Artisanal Scheme	47
	The Cooperative Scheme	47
	The Individualistic Scheme	48
	How to Get the Cash inside Somalia to Prepare an Operation	48
	Financiers Abroad	49
	Notes	50
Chapter 6	How Are the Proceeds Moved?	51
	Financial Wire Transfers	51
	Trade-Based Money Laundering	53
	Misuse of Money or Value Transfer Services (MVTS)	54
	Cross-Border Cash Smuggling	55
	Looking Forward: New Trends in Moving Money to and from Somalia	56
	Notes	57
Chapter 7	How Do Pirate Financiers Invest Their Proceeds?	59
	Overview of Reported Pirate Financiers' Investments within Somalia	59
	Investments in Legitimate Business Activities	61
	Pirate Financiers Using Their Proceeds for Other Criminal Activities	62
	Pirate Financiers Engaging in Smuggling and Trafficking	66
	Notes	67
Chapter 8	Khat and Real Estate	71
	Khat	71
	Khat Trade in Kenya	71
	Piracy and Khat	72

	The Real Estate Market	73
	Piracy Financial Flows and Real Estate	73
	Suspicion of Ransom Payments in the Real Estate Sector	74
	Notes	75

Section III **Conclusion** **77**

Chapter 9 Main Findings and Recommendations for Policy Engagement 79
Main Recommendations 81

Appendix A Human Trafficking Case Studies 85

Appendix B Khat Business 87

Appendix C Real Estate Boom 91

Glossary *95*

Bibliography *101*

Box
1.1	Interviews with Two Pirates	11

Figures
ES.1	Financial Flows of Proceeds of Piracy	1
II.1	Following the Money	38
4.1	Ships Successfully Hijacked	41
4.2	Evolution of Ransoms: Annual Amounts Collected by Somali Pirates in Ransom for Vessels and/or Crews Kidnapped between 2005 and 2012	42
4.3	Average Amount of Ransom Payments	43
4.4	Stocks and Flows of Ships Held and Released	44
5.1	False Invoicing to Finance Pirate Operations	49
6.1	Overinvoicing Scheme without an Intermediary	53
6.2	Overinvoicing Scheme with an Intermediary	54
7.1	Number of Investors Engaging in Activity	61
7.2	Number of Pirate Financiers Engaging in Activity North and South of Galkayo	63
B.1	Money Flows and the Distribution Network Associated with Khat	87

Maps

I.1	Map of Somalia	8
2.1	Regional Map	19
3.1	Evolution of the Main Pirate Networks until Today	31
7.1	Reported Locations of Pirate Financiers' Assets in Eastern Africa	60

Table

C.1	Credit to Private Sector (with Focus on Real Estate Sector)	92

Acknowledgments

This study, *Pirate Trails: Tracking the Illicit Financial Flows from Pirate Activities off the Horn of Africa*, has been, in all aspects, a collaborative endeavor among three diverse organizations—the World Bank, the United Nations Office on Drugs and Crime (UNODC), and the International Criminal Police Organization (INTERPOL). Its fruition was made possible through the expertise and contribution of many talented individuals.

This study was written by Stuart Yikona (Task Team Leader, Financial Market Integrity Service Line, World Bank),[1] Kevin M. Stephenson (Egmont Group Secretariat), Julian Casal (Latin America Region, World Bank), Francisca Maryanne U. Fernando (Financial Market Integrity Service Line, World Bank), Clément Gorrissen and David Lamair (both of the UNODC Global Programme against Money Laundering, Proceeds of Crime and the Financing of Terrorism [GPML]),[2] and George Lenny Kisaka (INTERPOL).

We would like to express our gratitude to the Government of Norway, the Foreign and Commonwealth Office of the United Kingdom, and the Government of the Netherlands for their generous financial support.

We are especially grateful to Bella Bird (Country Director, Somalia), Jean Pesme (Manager, Financial Market Integrity Service Line, Financial and Private Sector Development Network, and Coordinator, Stolen Asset Recovery [StAR] Initiative), Jennifer Bramlette (Programme Manager and Senior Advisor, Global Programme against Money Laundering, Proceeds of Crime and the Financing of Terrorism, UNODC, and a peer reviewer), Pierre St Hilarie (Assistant Director, Maritime Piracy Task Force, INTERPOL, and a peer reviewer), Stephen Platt (Stephen Platt & Associates LLP), and Anja Korenblik, (Programme Management Officer, Studies and Threat Analysis Section, UNODC) for their support and guidance on the project.

The invaluable support received from Quy-Toan Do (Senior Economist, World Bank, a peer reviewer) and Lin Ma (PhD Candidate, University of

---

1. Stuart Yikona took over the leadership of the project from Kevin Stephenson following Stephenson's departure from the World Bank in September 2012.

2. Clément Gorrissen conducted the UNODC scoping field research in November 2011, which also fed into the information used for this joint report.

Michigan) in developing and analyzing the joint UNODC–World Bank dataset on ransom payments sets an encouraging precedent in terms of genuine, efficient, and constructive cooperation on data collecting and analyzing between two international organizations. We are also grateful to Cyrus Mody of the International Maritime Bureau (IMB) for making available the dataset on piracy-related incidents compiled and maintained by the Piracy Reporting Center of the IMB; Louise Bosetti (Associate Expert, UNODC) for her very helpful comments on the joint UNODC–World Bank database; and Kristina Kuttnig and Deniz Mermerci from the UNODC Studies and Threat Analysis Section for their support in drafting the maps for this study. We also acknowledge the support provided by BridgeWing Solution GmBH of Zurich.

Heartfelt thanks are extended to our peer reviewers including Bernard Harborne and Michael Olavi Engman (both of the World Bank) and Per Gullestrap (Clipper Shipping). Each of the peer reviewers has brought a unique body of knowledge as well as distinct expertise in providing valuable insight that has strengthened the analysis in this study. We are indebted to them for their content suggestions including, most importantly, on the recommendations on how to address the monitoring and interdiction of illicit flows from pirate activities off the coast of Somalia.

The authors also benefited from helpful and insightful comments from Abdallah Abdallah (Africa Development Bank); Abdillahi Ismael (State University of Djibouti); Simon Marshall (Regional Anti-Piracy Prosecutions and Intelligence Coordinating Center); Jeanette Hauch, Samuel Munzele Maimbo, Matthias Mayr, Thilasoni Benjamin Musuku, Consolate K. Rusagara, Francesco Strobbe, Jack Titsworth, Emiko Todoroki, Carlos Leonardo Vincente, Cari Votava, Simon Christopher Walley, Emile van der Does de Willebois, Ji Won, and Yee Man Yu (all of the World Bank); and Andrew Weinschenck (U.S. Department of State), for which we are grateful.

Our gratitude is also extended to Working Group 5 of the Contact Group on Piracy off the Coast of Somalia, which gave us the mandate to undertake this study. Their support throughout this process has culminated in the publication of this report.

Our appreciation goes to the Governments of Djibouti, Ethiopia, Kenya, the Seychelles, and Somalia (Puntland and Federal authorities) for their cooperation and assistance during our visits to their respective countries. In particular, we would like to thank the agencies visited including the ministries of finance, foreign affairs, home affairs (internal security), the police, central banks, financial intelligence units, port authorities, private sector players, the diplomatic community, and the customs and revenue authorities.

The stellar work of our editor, Diane Stamm, is greatly appreciated. Special thanks are extended to Michael Geller for his support in the administration of the project. The support of Abdia Mohamed and Cindy Fisher of the World Bank Group's Publishing and Knowledge Division is appreciated.

Acknowledgments

Finally, we would like to extend our appreciation to our colleagues in the communications team for their guidance in the publication and launch of this study: Mary Elizabeth Donaldson, Nicole Frost, Richard Miron, Xenia Zia Morales, and Liudmila Uvarova (all of the World Bank).

The findings, interpretations, and conclusions expressed in this report are entirely those of the authors. They do not necessarily reflect the views of the World Bank, its Executive Directors, or the governments they represent, or those of the United Nations, the Secretariat of the United Nations, or its member states concerning the legal status of any country, territory, city, or area of its authorities, or those of INTERPOL and its member states.

We hope this report contributes to an understanding of the problem of piracy off the Horn of Africa and of the illicit financial flows that result from these activities. There is still much work to be done in addressing these phenomena.

Stuart Makanka Yikona
Task Team Leader
Financial Market Integrity Service Line
The World Bank

Contributors

Julian Casal is an operations officer in the Development Effectiveness Unit in the Latin America and the Caribbean Region of the World Bank. Prior to joining the Bank, Julian worked as an economist with the U.S. Treasury Department, where he was responsible for monitoring macroeconomic, fiscal, and financial matters in a portfolio of countries in Central and Southeast Asia. Julian received a master's degree in development and government from Georgetown University and a bachelor's degree in Latin American studies and economics from McGill University.

Francisca Maryanne Udeshika Fernando is a junior professional associate for the Stolen Asset Recovery (StAR) Initiative, a joint initiative of the World Bank and the United Nations Organization on Drugs and Crime, and with the Financial Market Integrity Service Line of the World Bank. Hailing from the Seychelles, an island nation that is greatly affected by piracy in the region, she has had work experience in the Ministry of Foreign Affairs in the Seychelles on issues relating to Somali piracy and her master's thesis focused on the issue of Somalia piracy for the Seychelles. She received her master of laws from the University of Toronto and her bachelor of laws from the London School of Economics and Political Science, where she was the Jones Markham Scholar. She is called to the Bar of England and Wales.

Clément Gorrissen is a consultant with the United Nations Office on Drugs and Crime (UNODC). In his current position, he helps coordinate and develop the UNODC activities in the Horn of Africa, with a specific focus on money or value transfer services. Prior to joining UNODC in 2010, he worked with the Bureau for Crisis Prevention and Recovery (BCPR) of the United Nations Development Programme (UNDP) in Geneva and then with UNDP Somalia. He graduated from Science-Po Lille, receiving his master's degree on Conflict Analysis and Peace Building following a master's thesis titled "The Conflict in Western Sahara, Conflicting Interests and Conflicting Identities." He is currently pursuing a PhD on financial flows in conflict-affected zones with the VU University of Amsterdam, The Netherlands.

George Lenny Kisaka is a regional specialized officer at the INTERPOL Regional Bureau of Eastern Africa in Nairobi. He is in charge of the Economic and

Financial Crimes coordination and police cooperation in 13 INTERPOL member countries in the region, including Somalia. In his current position, he is responsible for law enforcement initiatives in combating transnational crimes in the field of corruption, illicit trade, counterfeit currency, money laundering, terrorism financing, payment card frauds, and other new payment methods. He is also a member of the INTERPOL Maritime Piracy Task Force. Prior to joining INTERPOL, he worked at the Central Bank of Kenya as a Bank Fraud Detective in the area of financial intelligence and investigation for 10 years. He has a bachelor of education degree from Moi University, Kenya.

David Lamair is a United Nations Organization on Drugs and Crime adviser in the Eastern Africa Regional Office in Nairobi and is responsible for the areas of anti-money laundering and piracy financial flows. For most of the last decade he worked for the European Police Force in The Netherlands, where he was an intelligence analyst and carried out analytical and coordination roles in support of international investigations of organized crime. Prior to joining the European Police Force, he worked for five years as an intelligence analyst for the Belgian Federal Police and was a marketing research professor at a local training institute. He received his master's degree in business administration from the European University College, Brussels.

Kevin Mark Stephenson is a senior financial sector specialist, Financial Market Integrity Service Line of the Financial and Private Sector Vice Presidency of the World Bank, and is currently serving as the executive secretary of the Egmont Group of Financial Intelligence Units. He worked for the U.S. government serving as a special agent, Department of Treasury, U.S. Customs Service, and served as an attaché in American embassies in Skopje, the former Yugoslav Republic of Macedonia; Berlin, Germany; and New Delhi, India; he investigated money laundering, terrorist financing, drug smuggling, fraud, cyber-crimes, general smuggling, and other criminal offenses. He also served as the director of the Financial Intelligence Centre for the United Nations Interim Administration Mission in Kosovo, combating money laundering and terrorism financing. He served as the United Nations Integrated Mission in Timor-Leste anti-corruption advisor to the East Timor prime minister, advocating for transparency, accountability, and combating corruption. He received his master's degree from the University of Tennessee.

Stuart Makanka Yikona is a senior financial sector specialist in the Financial Market Integrity Service Line of the Financial and Private Sector Vice Presidency of the World Bank. Prior to joining the World Bank in June 2005, he worked as a consulting counsel with the Legal Department of the International Monetary Fund from 2001–05. In his current position, he advises client countries on issues related to combating financial crimes such as corruption and the laundering of proceeds of crimes; delivering capacity building programs to strengthen client countries' capacity to combat financial crimes; and most recently, pursuing research on the impact of ill-gotten money on the economy. He coauthored the report on *Ill-gotten Money and the Economy, Experiences from Malawi and Namibia* (2011). He received his master of laws from the University of London and completed his doctor of juridical science (SJD) in banking law at the University of Virginia Law School with "Insiders and Insider Abuse in Banking Institutions in the United States and Zambia."

Abbreviations

AMISOM	African Union Mission in Somalia
AML	anti-money laundering
CBK	Central Bank of Kenya
CDD	customer due diligence
CFT	combating the financing of terrorism
CGPCS	Contact Group on Piracy off the Coast of Somalia
COMESA	Common Market for Eastern and Southern Africa
CPIA	Country Policy and Institutional Assessment
ESAAMG	Eastern and Southern African Anti-Money Laundering Group
EU	European Union
EUNAVFOR	European Union Naval Force (also known as Operation Atalanta)
FATF	Financial Action Task Force (on money laundering)
FIU	financial intelligence unit
GDP	gross domestic product
HHN	Hobyo-Xarardheere Network
ICC	International Chamber of Commerce
IGAD	Intergovernmental Authority on Development
IMB	International Maritime Bureau
IMB PRC	International Maritime Bureau Piracy Reporting Centre
IMF	International Monetary Fund
INTERPOL	International Criminal Police Organization
KRA	Kenya Revenue Authority
KYC	know your customer
MENAFATF	Middle East and Northern Africa Financial Action Task Force
ML	money laundering
MVTS	money or value transfer services
NATO	North Atlantic Treaty Organisation
NGO	nongovernmental organization
OC	organized crime

OECD	Organisation for Economic Co-operation and Development
OFAC	Office of Foreign Assets Control (in the United States)
PAG	pirate action group
PIN	personal identification number
PIRI	Prime International Residential Index
RAPPICC	Regional Anti-Piracy Prosecution Intelligence Coordination Centre
RPGs	rocket-propelled grenades
SDN List	Specially Designated Nationals List
SIM	subscriber identity module
TF	terrorist financing
UAE	United Arab Emirates
UK	United Kingdom
UNCLOS	United Nations Convention on Law of the Sea
UNDP	United Nations Development Program
UNHCR	United Nations High Commission for Refugees
UNODC	United Nations Office on Drugs and Crime
USA	United States of America
WB	World Bank

Executive Summary

It is estimated that US$339 million to US$413 million was claimed in ransoms between April 2005 and December 2012 for pirate acts off the Horn of Africa. Twenty-first century piracy in this region has developed as a violent criminal act, which not only affects the victims but also has an impact on the region and the global economy.

This study on tracking the financial flows from proceeds of piracy attempts to follow what happens to the ransom monies. Figure ES.1 graphically summarizes this analysis of the flow of proceeds of piracy from the moment a ransom is paid.

Figure ES.1 Financial Flows of Proceeds of Piracy

At the top of the hierarchy displayed in figure ES.1 is "Ransom." Once received, the money filters down through the "system" to fund the activities of pirates and pirate financiers, which include acts of piracy, and various other criminal and business activities, including buying into the khat trade and human trafficking. Specifically, the ransom is distributed among the relevant stakeholders—the pirates involved with the capture of the ship (the pirate action group); the local community that has provided services to the pirates; and the pirate financiers who, having invested in the pirate operation, will receive the bulk of the ransom monies. The ransom monies are then moved through and around Somalia and the region, and invested in other sectors of the region's economy and also reinvested back into the Somali piracy business model. In that regard, piracy is sustained and reinforced through the proceeds of piracy.

While a significant focus by the international community has been on dealing with piracy through counterpiracy operations that include naval, air, and military operations, this study attempts to understand the illicit financial flows from the proceeds of piracy.

The study was conducted through a collaborative effort of the International Criminal Police Organization (INTERPOL), the United Nations Office on Drugs and Crime (UNODC), and the World Bank. Its focus is on financial flows and how such flows can be monitored by relevant law enforcement agencies. It complements another study done exclusively by the World Bank (referenced in this study as the World Bank Report) that assesses the economic costs of piracy off the coast of Somalia.

Using financial and economic data, and garnering evidence from interviews with relevant stakeholders who are or have been involved with piracy and other regional actors, the study attempts to assess how the proceeds are moved, invested, and used. Country visits were made to the region and outside the region to meet and talk with stakeholders including Somali pirates, law enforcement and military officials, regional government officials, financial analysts, central bank officials, commercial banking officials, money remitters, revenue agencies, and others such as real estate agents, and farmers and dealers in the khat business. The information learned in these interviews was combined with analysis of several open and closed sources and documents that are referenced throughout this study.

In conducting research of this nature, it was recognized that necessary data might not be available and that, even if available, might be difficult to obtain or even unreliable. As a consequence of this challenge, the team made a special effort to obtain information from all available, credible, open sources, and to engage as many stakeholders as possible. The data collected are sufficient to conduct credible analysis, but important gaps still remain and more critical research is necessary.

Somali Piracy: Criminal Networks

The evolution of Somali piracy networks can be broken down into three periods: pre-2008, 2008 to the end of 2010, and 2010 to the present. These three periods can be roughly associated to (a) the development of piracy from an amateurs' business to an organized activity, (b) the development of new competitors in the pirate business, and (c) piracy involving organized networks with members operating in different countries. Increased pressure from maritime forces and reduced success at sea has pushed these networks to move along the coast and become increasingly organized.

The study assesses the Somali piracy business models based on the different methods of financing and sharing the proceeds of a piracy operation, from the artisanal and individualistic scheme, involving a limited number of actors, to the more sophisticated cooperative scheme involving several shareholders and an organized chain of command.

Distributing the Proceeds

Negotiations for ransoms and the payment of the ransoms are usually shrouded in secrecy. Once received, it is payday for the pirates, the financiers of the pirate operation, and the local community who provide services to the pirates. Low-level pirates typically receive a standard fee of between US$30,000 and US$75,000 (which would amount to about 0.01–0.025 percent of an average ransom payment). They report using the monies to buy khat, alcohol, and expensive cars. The pirate financiers who invested in the piracy operations receive the bulk of the ransom, an estimated 30–75 percent of the total ransom payment depending on the Somali piracy business model.

Moving the Proceeds

Upon receipt, the ransom payments can be moved by financial transfer. In particular, Djibouti, Kenya, and the United Arab Emirates have been identified as three of the main transit points for financial operations leaving and entering Somalia. A greater portion of the ransom payments is invested locally than expected. It appears that most of the money is typically moved by cross-border cash smuggling, made easy by the high porosity of the regional borders and trade-based money laundering. There are also concerns that the services of money or value transfer services (MVTS) are also being misused to move monies outside of Somalia, and the sector needs support to cope with such abuses of its services.

Investing the Proceeds of Piracy

In order to launder proceeds, financiers can buy into legitimate business interests. The study does a deeper dive analysis of two sectors, in particular—the khat industry and the real estate market. Given the lucrative nature of the khat trade, which is a predominantly cash-based business, the culture of khat chewing in Somalia, and control that Somalis have over the distribution network of the khat trade, there is evidence suggesting that pirates are increasingly buying into this network.

The perception on the ground would also suggest that pirates invest heavily in real estate in the region. However, the findings of the study could not point at precise estates or precise buildings into which ransom payments had been invested. To that extent, there is little to no information available to support allegations of a causal link between piracy and increased real estate prices in some countries in the region. Further research is needed to understand who and what are the drivers of the real estate boom in the region.

Other legitimate businesses in trade (for example, trade in petroleum), transportation, and the services industry (for example, restaurants and hotels), also offer viable opportunities for the pirates to invest the proceeds from piracy.

A greater concern is how ransom money may be fueling other criminal activities, apart from piracy, in the region. Some pirate financiers are engaging in human trafficking, including migrant smuggling, and investing in militias and military capacities on land in Somalia. It would be a challenge to prove each and every such allegation, and most reports received by the team are subject to a confidential attribution, due to the secrecy of ongoing investigations. However, the fact that proceeds from piracy are being used to perpetuate other criminal activities is concerning for the development and stability of the region as a whole, and deserves increased attention from local and international stakeholders.

The number of ships still being used as mother ships is very limited, and no fishing vessels were being held at anchorage by Somali pirates at the time of finalizing this study. Furthermore, the naval operations in the region are increasingly costly, and it is important to consider alternative measures to combatting the piracy problem to include monitoring of financial flows.

Against this background, we offer five key recommendations for consideration by practitioners (on an operational level) and policy makers, including those in the donor community. These actions would significantly contribute to mitigating the risks associated with the financial flows from piracy within the region and beyond.

Main Recommendations

Regional Cooperation and Collaboration

There is need for a strong commitment by countries in the region to work together to monitor financial flows from criminal activities, including acts of piracy. They should adopt policies and procedures that encourage cooperation, collaboration, and information sharing among all competent authorities within countries and across the region. These countries should adopt and implement comprehensive strategic plans targeting the proceeds of crime and provide sufficient resources and training to the competent authorities to trace, interdict, freeze, seize, and ultimately confiscate the proceeds of crime. To improve the capacity of the competent authorities in the region to combat the illicit flows from piracy, experienced jurisdictions should provide assistance and training. Moreover, it is important to enhance the level of trust and communication among competent authorities across borders, so that intelligence and other data can be shared in real time and in order to improve multiagency coordination.

Dealing with Cross-Border Cash Smuggling

A large part of the ransom money procured by pirates is moved in cash by air, land, or sea. Therefore, improving the capacity of countries in the Horn of Africa to adequately target, interdict, seize, and ultimately confiscate illegal cross-border cash smuggling is paramount to any strategy aimed at tackling the issue of financial flows linked to piracy. Ways in which to do this include developing and enhancing channels to exchange information between customs and border authorities, and improving human, material, and technological capacities, for example, through investing in new technology and developing proper interdiction techniques.

Strengthen Money or Value Transfer Service (MVTS) Providers against Criminal Abuses

Development of an appropriate and proportional oversight framework of Somali MVTS operations in Somalia, and improving cooperation and information sharing with law enforcement agencies in countries where they operate will enable authorities to promote a safe and transparent sector and protect them from abuse, while promoting financial inclusion. The oversight framework needs to be proportionate to Somalia's situation, because overregulation would hinder the critical role MVTS play in Somali society. Discussions between Somali MVTS and the Somali Government should serve as a basis to ensure a right balance is being struck in that respect. Such seed work will be paramount to the future development of a proper Anti-Money Laundering and Combating the Financing of Terrorism regulatory and enforcement regime framework for Somalia. Oversight of MVTS operations within each country in the region; self-regulation by MVTS themselves; and risk-based, tailored solutions to protect MVTS from abuse are all the more relevant in the region, given the importance of remittances from a development perspective. The ultimate goal should be to allow and help these actors to take a more risk-based approach in the conduct of their activities, thereby ensuring that the activities take place in a legal, transparent, competitive, and respectable environment that takes account of both the private sector's and its clients' interests, and the needs of law enforcement agencies.

Increase Monitoring of Production and Trade in Khat in Kenya and Beyond

The lack of transparency of the khat business in Kenya makes the business susceptible to abuse by criminal networks. Developing an appropriate monitoring mechanism by Kenya would assist the authorities in understanding the financial flows from acts of piracy into the khat industry. The regulatory framework for the khat trade in Djibouti, Ethiopia, and Somaliland can serve as a benchmark for Kenya.

Enhance Data Collection and Monitoring of the Real Estate Sector in Countries in the Region

Better data collection on financing of real estate transactions will enable countries in the region to know and understand the various financing methods in the purchase of real estate. It will be critical to have a proper classification of the sources of financing real estate, proper due diligence of parties to transactions, promotion of the use of the banking system when engaging in real estate transactions, and in so doing, the authorities may be better able to monitor the financial inflows and outflows in the real estate sector.

Such monitoring will enable the authorities and the public to avoid making assumptions that are not backed by accurate estimates of financial flows into the sector, that is, what flows are attributable to dirty money such as proceeds of piracy.

SECTION I

Introduction

Map I.1 Map of Somalia

Source: © United Nations. Used with permission; further permission required for re-use.

CHAPTER 1

"I Am a Pirate"

"It is not written on the bills if the money is haram [illegal] *or not."*[1]

It is estimated that US$339 million to US$413 million was claimed in ransoms for pirate acts off the coast of Somalia and the Horn of Africa between April 2005 and December 2012. Piracy is a crime, and often a very violent crime, which has implications not only for its victims but which also affects the international shipping and trade routes in the area and, consequently, the regional and global economy.

This study, by the International Criminal Police Organization (INTERPOL), United Nations Office on Drugs and Crime (UNODC), and the World Bank, attempts to understand the illicit financial flows from these piracy activities off the Coast of Somalia and the Horn of Africa. It complements the study conducted exclusively by the World Bank that looks at the economic costs of piracy (referred to in this study as the World Bank Report).

Why This Study?

Up until now, little attention has been paid to tracking and disrupting the financial flows from piracy. There has been significant focus on securing the ships that pass through Somali waters and, where apprehended, prosecuting and incarcerating the captured pirates. The global community has not been successful in taking collective action to track, detect, disrupt, and confiscate the proceeds of piracy.

In that vein, the primary objective of this study is to add to the existing knowledge about piracy activities off the coast of Somalia and, more specifically, the illicit financial flows it generates. The focus is on the structure of the flows and, more important, on helping to design appropriate responses to address the problem in a holistic manner. The study sought to identify the flow of funds through the piracy operational chain, and through analysis of financial and economic data on how the proceeds of piracy are used and are moved through and out of the region and the destinations of these proceeds.

The study considers areas of vulnerability, from legislative and operational perspectives, within the concerned jurisdictions' framework to combat dirty money as it relates to the flows of illicit proceeds generated by piracy. Moreover, the study identifies where collective action (particularly at the regional level) would be critical to having a meaningful impact, including identifying opportunities for strategic collaboration, and possible platforms for regional cooperation to build the capacity of relevant public sector agencies to monitor these financial flows.

Pirate Financiers and Pirates

Modern-day Somali pirates are organized into groups, mainly along clan lines, and operate as criminal units. The patterns of operation and organization of these groups vary, but most are armed with rocket-propelled grenades, AK-47, and tracking devices. The pirates hijack and hold hostage vessels, cargos, and crews in exchange for ransoms.

Pirates engage in criminal acts for the money—money that is then typically spent on alcohol, khat,[2] and prostitutes. Proceeds from piracy are also reinvested into the financing of future pirate operations and may support the purchase of real estate, investment in the khat trade, and other business investments and ventures. Somali piracy has evolved into a transnational model—from small-scale, locally executed and funded operations into a transnational network with flows of funds, operatives, and resources coming from abroad and proceeds flowing elsewhere.

As stated by U.S. Attorney Neil MacBride in a 2012 case concerning the Somali pirate negotiator Mohammad Saaili Shibin[3]:

> I think this case explodes the myth ... that pirates are some kind of romantic swashbuckling characters from Hollywood summer movies. This case showed that pirates are brutal, greedy, reckless, desperate criminals who will kidnap, torture and ultimately kill hostages in pursuit of their financial greed.

During the research for this study, the team interviewed over 30 individuals involved in piracy activities off the coast of Somalia. The primary focus of the interviews was to discover where the money went after ransoms were paid. Even though many of the pirates interviewed were not mid- or high-level pirate financiers, but mainly crewmen who were sent out on the high seas to hunt and hijack ships, many were paid ransoms, many spent ransom money, and many had information about what the pirate financiers did with the larger ransom payments.

To protect the identities and safety of these pirates, this study does not use their names or provide specific details that might jeopardize their safety. Of the 30-odd pirates interviewed by the team, three convicted pirates distinguished themselves as the most accessible and cooperative and were willing to be interviewed by the team over two days.

The Pirates Talk…

Their stories were similar. They were all born and raised in Somalia and had never traveled outside the country of Somalia except for their adventures on the high seas. They got involved in piracy for one simple reason: money. They made no excuses; it was their decision to become pirates. They had never truly experienced safety or security, and the political and economic situation in Somalia provided little opportunity for people to find sustainable employment. Although many of the pirates felt they had very limited opportunities, they clearly stated that becoming a pirate was their choice, and a bad choice, at that.

Box 1.1 captures the experiences of two of the pirates who spoke with the team. Although these are the comments of only two pirates, they echo a common refrain expressed by other pirates; that is, that they got involved with piracy activities because they were attracted by the money offered to and spent on them.

Box 1.1 Interviews with Two Pirates

Pirate 1

"I was an unemployed, occasional fisherman and someone approached me. Had I been involved in a decent job at that time, I would have never got close to that. The man promised me money and khat. He explained how he got his wealth. The man was my cousin. He was a successful pirate and was accompanied by an investor. He brought me from Mogadishu to Bossaaso by car.

"They took care of me in Bossaaso. I used to get everything on my cousin's name—khat, comfort… I lived that life for two to three weeks. I was living like a Minister. The financier brought a car and took us to Garacad. We stayed there for two months. We were living like vampires: only at night. Sleeping the whole day, chewing khat the rest of the time … they were awaiting on another boat.

"It was in January this year. Then we went at sea, and got arrested by a British vessel. Somehow it was an escape. For two weeks, the only things I could see were the sky, the sea, the sky, the sea. And I was telling myself: 'What was I thinking?!' When I saw the Brits, I was happy…"

Pirate 2

"I was a fisherman in Mogadishu. It used to be a fairly good business, but it became difficult and unsafe over time. In 2005, I reached Xarardheere where piracy had started. I tried my best not to be a pirate. My friends and I used to help each other, borrow from each other, and lend money to each other.

"I struggled… as times got more and more difficult. But as my friends turned to piracy, they started to refuse lending me money. They were saying: We are working to get that money. Why don't you do the same?"

"With piracy everything became more and more expensive… A liter of fuel was already US$100. So just try and imagine how much a liter of milk was. Then the diaspora would send less money to families and clans with pirates among them. So the others could not catch up. And my Mom was still sick. I couldn't feed my family properly. That's when I eventually joined piracy."

Key Terms Used in the Study

The glossary provides definitions of the terms used in this study, but here we define several of the key terms:

Piracy. The definition of piracy used in this study is the same as the one used in Article 101 of the United Nations Convention on the Law of the Sea (UNCLOS) 1982. Under that convention, Piracy consists of any of the following acts:

Any illegal acts of violence or detention, or any act of depredation, committed for private ends by the crew or the passengers of a private ship or a private aircraft, and directed:

1. On the high seas, against another ship or aircraft, or against persons or property on board such ship or aircraft.
2. Against a ship, aircraft, persons or property in a place outside the jurisdiction of any State.

Any act of voluntary participation in the operation of a ship or of an aircraft with knowledge of facts making it a pirate ship or aircraft.

Any act of inciting or of intentionally facilitating an act described in subparagraph (a) or (b).

Contact Group on Piracy off the Coast of Somalia. The Contact Group on Piracy off the Coast of Somalia (CGPCS) brings together all international actors, governmental and nongovernmental, willing to engage in fighting piracy off the coast of Somalia. The CGPCS was established pursuant to the United Nations Security Council 1851 (2008) on January 14, 2009. The CGPCS is divided into the following five Working Groups:

1. Working Group 1, chaired by the United Kingdom, is in charge of naval coordination.
2. Working Group 2, chaired by Denmark, is in charge of legal issues.
3. Working Group 3, chaired by the Republic of Korea, is in charge of making the liaison between governments and the private sector.
4. Working Group 4 is chaired by Egypt and focuses on public campaigns, raising awareness about the problems and danger of piracy.
5. Working Group 5 is chaired by Italy and is in charge of tackling the issue of illicit financial flows related to piracy. Established in late 2011 following the plenary session of the CGPCS, it is the last Working Group created.

Pirate. A pirate is a person who is said to have committed any acts that constitute an act of piracy (as defined above). For the purpose of this study, the focus is on "Somali pirates," that is, Somali piracy mainly occurring off the coast of Somalia and the Horn of Africa. The focus of this study is on the "pirate" who is engaged in such acts of piracy off the coast of Somalia and the Horn of Africa. These are acts, committed in the Arabian Sea and the Gulf of Oman by individuals whose land base is on the coast of Somalia or in the Somali hinterland.

Pirate Financiers. Pirate financiers (also referred to as "investors" in this study) are persons who invest in pirate activities. They are the focus of this study, since they receive the bulk of ransom payments, which are then moved in and out of Somalia and invested into other activities and businesses. Under UNCLOS, they can be charged with piracy for "inciting or intentionally facilitating illegal acts of violence and detention directed against ship, aircraft, persons or property on the high seas."

Fragile State or Situation. While there is no general consensus on the definition of a "fragile state," the term generally denotes those periods when states or institutions lack the capacity, accountability, or legitimacy to mediate relations between citizen groups and between citizens and the state, making them vulnerable to violence. For the purpose of this study, and in general, Somalia is considered a fragile state.

Financial Flows. For the purpose of this study, financial flows include the money that flows primarily through remitters, cross-border movement, mobile banking, wire transfers, and Money or Value Transfer Services (MVTS), as well as informal flows through bulk cash smuggling and other illicit (underground) money remitters.

Khat. Khat (also commonly referenced to as *qat, qaad, gat, jaad, tchat,* and *miraa*) is a small leafy plant. Among communities in the Horn of Africa, the Arabian Peninsula, and in particular in Somalia, the chewing of khat is a social custom dating back many thousands of years. The khat trade in this region is worth hundreds of millions of dollars a year.

Money Laundering (ML). Money laundering is the process by which proceeds from a criminal activity are disguised to conceal their illicit origins. Most countries subscribe to the legal definition of money laundering as found in the United Nations Convention Against Illicit Traffic in Narcotic Drugs and Psychotropic Substances (1988) (Vienna Convention) and the United Nations Convention Against Transnational Organized Crime (2000) (Palermo Convention).[4]

The Somali Piracy Business Model. This study analyzes the Somali piracy business model through the criminal networks and the way pirates manage and move their proceeds. These various piracy networks have their own historical developments and are ever evolving "organizations." The study highlights three dominant models of financing an operation and sharing the proceeds—which one could call "business models" for ease of reference, namely (a) the "artisanal" scheme, (b) the "cooperative" scheme, and (c) the individualistic scheme (Do et al. 2013),[5] all of which will be explained in detail in the upcoming chapters.

The Team. Refers to the project team that conducted this study, comprising staff from the International Criminal Police Organization (INTERPOL), the United Nations Office on Drugs and Crime (UNODC), and the World Bank.

World Bank Report. Refers to a World Bank report on the economic aspects of piracy titled, "Pirates of Somalia: Ending the Threat, Rebuilding a Nation" (World Bank 2013). The report shows that it is in the international community's common interest to find a resolution to Somali piracy and help the

Government of Somalia rebuild the country. The costs imposed by Somali pirates on the global economy are so high that international mobilization to eradicate piracy off the Horn of Africa not only has global security benefits, but also makes good economic sense.

Outline of the Study

The rest of this study is organized as follows.

Chapter 2 describes the context and audience for the study; explains the study's methodological framework, including information on what data sources were available; and identifies the challenges in undertaking the study. Chapter 3 provides background on the issues of pirate activities off the coast of Somalia and the Horn of Africa, and defines the problem of piracy and its origins. Section II then focuses on understanding the financial flows with respect to piracy activities. Chapter 4 looks at the ransoms paid to pirates, starting with negotiations of the ransoms and the volume of money involved. Then chapter 5 focuses on the distribution of proceeds from piracy to the various actors involved in supporting or carrying out pirate activities. Chapter 6 explores the ways in which proceeds are moved in and out of Somalia. Chapter 7 looks at how the financiers invest their proceeds. Following this analysis, chapter 8 focuses specifically on investment by piracy financiers in the khat business and real estate. In the final section III, chapter 9 of the study concludes with suggested areas for policy and operational engagement within the region and beyond.

Notes

1. Inmate interviewed by the team in Mombasa on August 7, 2012. The man was then awaiting trial on charges of piracy.
2. Khat is a small, leafy plant chewed to induce stimulation. Chewing khat is a social custom that dates back many thousands of years in this region of the Horn of Africa. Today, the khat trade is worth hundreds of millions of dollars a year. This study looks at the illicit financial flows of piracy through the khat trade, the details of which are described in chapter 8 of this report.
3. This refers to the case of Mohammad Saaili Shibin, who was tried, convicted, and sentenced to a dozen life sentences (New York Times 2012). (For the court record of the case, see Case No. 2:11-cr-00033: USA v. Shibin, http://www.plainsite.org/flashlight/case.html?id=1689934Shibin, Case 2:11-cr-00033-RGD-DEM Document 91 Filed April 27, 2012.)
4. "The conversion or transfer of property, knowing that such property is derived from any [drug trafficking] offense or offenses or from an act of participation in such offense or offenses, for the purpose of concealing or disguising the illicit origin of the property or of assisting any person who is involved in the commission of such an offense or offenses to evade the legal consequences of his actions; The concealment or disguise of the true nature, source, location, disposition, movement, rights with respect to, or ownership of property, knowing that such property is derived from an offense or offenses or from an act of participation in such an offense or offenses, and; the acquisition,

possession or use of property, knowing at the time of receipt that such property was derived from an offense or offenses or from an act of participation in such offense … or offenses" (Palermo Convention).

5. This World Bank Report on the economic aspects of piracy is offering a reduced form for the business model of pirate operations, in order to suggest an alternative business model for coastal areas. In this respect, the analysis developed uses analytical tools from economic theories in order to offer an alternative economic model. The approach taken by the present study adds another angle, since the analysis is focusing on the organized crime aspect of piracy. As explained in this report, the various networks operating have their own historical developments and are ever evolving "organizations." Consequently, by differentiating the various networks the analysis developed, this study is able to go to a more micro level, identifying three models of financing an operation and sharing the proceeds—which one could call "business models" for ease of reference.

CHAPTER 2

The Context for This Study

Audience

This study is directed to policy makers, and its key objective is to make them aware of the difficulties in detecting, tracking, disrupting, and confiscating the proceeds from piracy activities off the coast of Somalia. It seeks to encourage policy makers to take collective and individual action in strengthening processes and information-gathering mechanisms to track and disrupt such proceeds. Such action would enhance the capacity of law enforcement in the field.

This study is also aimed at financial sector regulators, money value transfer companies with links to the region, and other relevant public and private sector stakeholders. In addition, the study seeks to inform the international community—including nongovernmental organizations (NGOs), donors, and other international organizations involved in efforts to resolve the piracy problem within the region. In particular, the study hopes to contribute to the international forum of the Contact Group on Piracy off the Coast of Somalia (CGPCS), and to contribute to the ongoing discussions and coordination of actions among the 62 countries and international organizations of the CGPCS and its Working Group 5.

Methodological Framework

When preparing to conduct this study, it was determined that the best approach would be an all-inclusive one and to conduct the research in the broadest way possible. In addition, it was deemed necessary to apply a more experience-based approach to maximize learning via discoveries from the team's experiences during its research and field visits, including in Puntland, Somalia.

As mentioned, the team was composed of staff from three organizations—the World Bank, the United Nations Office on Drugs and Crime (UNODC), and the International Criminal Police Organization (INTERPOL)—to capitalize on the synergies from the combined expertise and resources of the three institutions.

Sources of Data

The findings of this study are based on information obtained during a series of structured interviews conducted by the team, on the analysis of available data, and on the views of stakeholders including both public and private sector officials. Given the scarcity of the available data, there was a need to cross check with multiple sources.

To conduct this extensive research, the team visited Somalia (Puntland[1]), Djibouti, Ethiopia, Kenya, the Seychelles (see map 2.1), Denmark, and the United Kingdom, where they met with relevant stakeholders and focused on obtaining as much relevant information as possible. Despite several efforts, the team was unable to visit the United Arab Emirates.

Some of the key actors interviewed were:

- *Convicted or reformed Somali pirates* (interviewed in Kenya, Puntland, and the Seychelles), who provided important insights into the organization of the pirate business, its market characteristics, the recruitment process and wage levels, financing of pirate operations, and channels (gatekeepers) through which financial flows are distributed to stakeholders within and between economies
- *Law enforcement and military officials*, who provided a deeper understanding of pirate operations to date
- *Victims*, including shipping companies and the law firms and consultants that represent them, which provided information on where, when, and how much ransom has been paid as a result of piracy activity off the coast of Somalia and method of payment
- *Officials*, from Ministries of Finance, Foreign Affairs, Justice, and Home Affairs, and other important stakeholders who provided information relevant to the goals of the study including existing threat assessments, intelligence reports, surveys, and other relevant information
- *Financial Intelligence Units (FIUs)*, which provided information on what measures are in place to monitor financial flows in the countries visited and on the actual flows themselves, when they were in a position to share such information
- *Central Banks* in Djibouti, Ethiopia, and Kenya, who provided the team with information on the measures already in place and planned to identify illicit flows, and relevant statistical material
- *Revenues and Customs authorities* who provided a better understanding of the flow of goods and cash coming into and also leaving Somalia to validate the origin/destination of goods and services and whether there were any reports of suspiciously large amounts of cash crossing borders
- *Money remitters*, who provided information on their role in remittance and money transfer within and between economies, their vulnerability to illicit flows including those from piracy, their size and capability in handling huge transfers, and most common destinations and origins of money transfers
- *Real estate agents, khat dealers and khat farmers, and other businesses*, which form an important trade link with Somalia and who provided a better understanding

Map 2.1 Regional Map

Source: © United Nations. Used with permission; further permission required for re-use.

of the profile of their clients, mode of payment including preferred currency and magnitude, location of most estates, and origin of goods
- *Other security and confidential sources*, from both the public and private sectors, which provided limited but crucial information.

The analysis contained in, and the conclusions drawn by, this study are largely based in part on the interviews with the above-mentioned stakeholders who contributed to the study's evaluation and understanding of the illicit flows of the proceeds from pirate activities. In addition, many policy makers, law enforcement agencies, and relevant stakeholders in the region and beyond who are involved in combating the piracy problem commented on the early drafts of the report.

The conclusions drawn from these interviews were combined with analysis of several open and closed sources and documents that are referenced throughout this study. In particular, information was obtained from, among others, the World Bank Report on the economic aspects of piracy, the Report of the United Nations Monitoring Group on Somalia and Eritrea, Central Bank annual reports, the World Bank–United Nations Office on Drug and Crime database on ransom payments, the United Nations Office on Drugs and Crime's dataset on pirate financiers, and newspaper and magazine reports on issues related or connected to piracy activities off the coast of Somalia.

Vulnerabilities

In conducting research of this nature, it was recognized that necessary data might not be available and that, even if available, might be difficult to obtain. To partially mitigate this risk, the team made a special effort to obtain information from all available, credible, open sources, and to engage as many different stakeholders as possible. At the same time, this multisource strategy addresses the possible problems with reliability of sources of information.

The study encountered the following challenges:

1. Because a large portion of this criminal activity occurred in a fragile state and in an environment with low levels of safety and security, access to sources of information by the team was very limited. Since piracy is a criminal act and takes place in secrecy, this is a challenging area to study.
2. The veil of secrecy surrounding negotiations and ransom payments was a serious impediment to gathering information both on the amounts of money generated by piracy and on the ways in which those amounts were transferred. The overall limited cooperation by the private sector with the team limited the team's access to information that had potential value to the study. However, certain elements of the private sector affected by piracy activities did cooperate with the team.
3. Because of the high level of secrecy in the piracy business, electronic transaction and audit trails are almost nonexistent. This is an extra impediment to tracking transactions related to ransoms with conventional technical means.

The Context for This Study 21

4. States in the region have little ability to control porous land and sea borders, which limits the availability of data about the movement of goods and people that could have been valuable to the team. The limited capacity of law enforcement to control the borders and collect data on how criminal proceeds move through the region limited the team's ability to identify the methods.
5. Of particular concern are the absence of laws specifically designed to combat illicit flows and the very limited capacity to enforce existing laws. Indeed, the frameworks to combat financial crime in the region are limited, and the reporting of suspicious financial transactions is absent or a very new requirement. Ongoing analysis and investigation or even litigation on money laundering or counterfinancing of terrorism would have been an interesting source of information on the laundering of proceeds of crime and ransom money.

These challenges forced the team to be creative in their methodological approach.

Methodological Adaptation and Mitigation of Risks

Faced with these multiple impediments to proper data collection on actual financial flows, the team decided to use the scenario analysis technique[2] to try to understand the piracy business model and the financial flows related to it.

The team also attempted to identify the vulnerabilities of the current regional states concerning law enforcement and institutional actions to trace the actual financial flows from criminal activities including from piracy activities.

Joint UNODC–World Bank Dataset on Pirate Ransoms

In addition, for the purpose of this study and that of the World Bank Report on the economic aspects of piracy, a joint dataset on the ransom amounts was developed, using sources from the International Maritime Bureau at the International Chamber of Commerce, the International Maritime Organization, the European Union Naval Force[3] (EUNAVFOR), several Member States' law enforcement agencies, several law firms and private security companies, and open sources. The dataset gathers most of the ransom amounts available, as well as details on the dates of hijacking and dates of release, the type of vessel, the ship owner and managers, the crew, and so forth. In the report, this joint UNODC–World Bank dataset is referred to as "UNODC-WB 2012."

The dataset gathers the amounts of 109 ransom payments over 154 cases between 2005 and 2012, where it is known that a vessel was hijacked and released against a ransom payment to Somali pirates. For the 55 cases where the amount is missing, a linear equation was used, taking into account factors such as the size of the vessel, the type of cargo, the duration of negotiations, and the size and nationality of the crew. When a covariate was missing, corresponding sample averages were used to replace the missing value. Based on that methodology, a low and a high estimate were produced. Low estimates only show results based on ransom amounts that were actually retrieved and entered into the database. High estimates take into account the amounts retrieved and the inputted amounts altogether. The average value of payments made during a year is based on the low estimate for the corresponding year.

UNODC Dataset on Pirate Financiers

Based on data gathered from open sources, confidential sources, private security sources, and interviews in the field, another dataset was developed, identifying and profiling the reported investments of over a hundred alleged pirate financiers. Data referenced from the dataset are referred to as "UNODC 2012" in the present report.

The original dataset developed information on 107 alleged pirate financiers, gathering information such as clan affiliations, reported investments, reported locations where assets are detained, main areas of operations, cases involved, and account or phone numbers when available. Due to the difficulty in finding such information, some cases are more detailed than others. This source document was used to extract information for the analysis of pirate financiers' investments and the map locating pirate financiers' assets in Somalia. In order to proceed with the analysis of pirate financiers' investments, it was decided to keep only those financiers for which reporting mentioned specific investments, beyond the financing of pirate operations. The sample used for that analysis comprised 59 cases whose investments were distributed in the following categories—keeping in mind that one pirate financier can engage in several different categories:

- Financial or accountant services for others: Some financiers do not limit their services only to investing in the setting up of pirate operations; they also provide direct services as accountants or investment advisors, or provide loans to other financiers looking to invest in a given operation.
- Various smuggling: While some pirate "foot soldiers" have acknowledged engaging in smuggling activities on top of their piracy activities, the number of pirate financiers also acting as human traffickers or migrant smugglers is less important. But this category also encompasses other smuggling activities such as drug smuggling and weapon smuggling.
- Development of militia/political influence: Given that the regions where pirate financiers have an influence are highly volatile politically and security-wise, it was chosen to merge these two categories since, on the one hand, one cannot have any political influence without military capacities and, on the other hand, the acquiring of military capacities automatically engenders political influence, either for oneself or to be used as mercenaries, thereby having a less direct but nonetheless effective political influence.
- Transports: Truck or bus rental, repair garage, oil station, or oil supply companies.
- Import/export: Any business involving the shipment or importation of commodities.
- Khat business.
- Farming activities (agricultural or livestock) and/or retail and selling of food products: These categories were merged since both potentially have a direct

link to piracy. Selling or producing food products will facilitate the provision of catering services to crews and foot soldiers involved in an operation. It is also a way to reduce the costs of a pirate operation, by having one of the related expenses (food and catering) being directly taken care of by the financier.
- Hotel/restaurants/other real estate.
- Various businesses or factories in Somalia or abroad: This category comprises small retail shops or small-scale businesses, as well as bigger joint ventures or even factories.

Notes

1. The formal name of Puntland is Puntland State of Somalia. It is located in northeastern Somalia, covers a third of Somalia's geographic area, and is home to about a third of the country's population. Its leaders declared it an autonomous region in 1998 and it is now part of the Federal State of Somalia.
2. Scenario analysis is a process of analyzing possible future events by considering alternative possible outcomes of the destination and use of financial flows from piracy.
3. Also known as Operation Atalanta.

CHAPTER 3

Background on Piracy

Origins of Somali Piracy

Piracy is an age-old crime; as far back as the days of Ancient Rome, Cicero "*declared pirates to be* hostis humani generi, *meaning the enemy of all mankind*" (Burgess 2006). From its ancient origins through its peak during the Middle Ages, piracy has affected the oceans and the seas from North America to the Caribbean to Africa and the Far East. In recent years, there has been a revival of piracy activities off the coast of Somalia and off the Gulf of Guinea. Piracy has once again come to the forefront as a global problem.

This study will focus on modern-day pirate activities off the coast of Somalia and the Horn of Africa. In light of this resurgence, the question arises as to why piracy has developed as a lucrative criminal enterprise in Somalia, in particular. Part of the answer lies in the fact that Somalia is a fragile state—one in which there is a dearth of capacity to provide for the security and well-being of a majority of the population. It is characterized by weak legal and institutional structures that are unable to provide basic goods and services to the population (OECD 2008).

Current Situation in Somalia

In September 2012, Somalia elected a new President of the Federal Republic of Somalia, Hassan Sheikh Mohamud, following the adoption of a new Constitution and new Parliament (UN Security Council Report, October 2012, 3, 4). Soon thereafter, President Mohamud and his government outlined their policy priorities for a new Somalia to include security stabilization, political outreach and reconciliation, and the delivery of basic services to the people (Mohamud 2012, 3). There was recognition of the Somali government for the first time in more than 20 years by important international partners such as the United States, the European Union, and the United Kingdom. The normalization of relations with other development partners such as the World Bank further strengthens the government's position and the positive outlook for Somalia.

Indeed, in keeping with the priorities outlined, the president has taken steps to address the problem of piracy off the coast of Somalia. He has done so by offering partial amnesty to low-level pirates or "foot soldiers" (CNN 2013). Underscoring the rationale for taking such action, the President declared that, "we have been negotiating with pirates indirectly through the elders to see if we can organize a partial amnesty for the young boys lured in this criminal activity" (CNN 2013). However, this amnesty does not extend to the pirate financiers or organizers.

Complementing the task of the new government has been concerted and coordinated actions taken by military assets from the North Atlantic Treaty Organization, the European Union Naval Force (EUNAVFOR), the Kenyan armed forces, and African Union Mission in Somalia (AMISOM) soldiers. As a result of these military efforts, incidents of piracy have plummeted and a measure of stability to areas of Southern Somalia has returned (UN Security Council Report, October 2012, 5, 6). Moreover, the actions of the AMISOM has significantly reduced the presence of Al-Shabaab in Southern Somalia, although it has continued, on various occasions, to launch attacks in Mogadishu (UN Security Council Report, October 2012, 5, 6).

Despite the progress that has been made in resolving the conflict in Somalia, the country remains in a fragile situation. Significant challenges remain in rebuilding Somalia's legal, institutional, and human capacity to enable the government to respond effectively to the needs and aspirations of its population. Moreover, in view of the challenges of fragility noted below, the recent progress remains extremely fragile, fluid, and uncertain, and only time will tell whether the progress can be sustained over the long term (World Bank 2013, 2).

Somalia, A Fragile State

There is no general consensus on the definition of a "fragile state," but broadly the term denotes a state in which the primary institutions of the state are unable to meet or manage the expectations of its population and capacity through the political process (OECD 2008). According to Stefan Wolff (2006), there seems to be a convergence of opinion that the term describes a range of phenomena associated with state weakness and failure, loss of territorial control, low administrative capacity, and political instability.

In its *World Development Report of 2011*, the World Bank expands its definition of fragility to mean "those periods when states or institutions lack the capacity, accountability, or legitimacy to mediate relations between citizen groups and between citizens and the state, making them vulnerable to violence" (WDR 2011, xvi). The World Bank, while recognizing the different criteria used to characterize fragility in a state, considers the term to refer to countries that are facing particularly severe development challenges such as weak governance, limited administrative capacity, violence, or the legacy of conflict (Global Monitoring Report 2007, 40; WDR 2011, 87–88).

According to this definition, and using the measure of the countries' Country Policy and Institutional Assessment (CPIA) and governance scores, Somalia is categorized as a state in a fragile situation (World Bank 2013).[1] Notwithstanding some of the progress that was made in 2012, Somalia is still characterized by ongoing conflict, no legitimate monopoly on the use of force, weak state-society and intrasociety relations, a high dependency on external humanitarian assistance and diaspora remittances, and substantial war economies such as piracy and arms trafficking (OECD 2011, 18, 19). Time will tell whether the new federal government will be able to exert its influence in Somalia and begin in small steps to reverse some of the challenges underlying its fragile situation (World Bank 2013).

Since the onset of the civil war in 1991, data collection in Somalia has been inconsistent and of variable quality. According to the *2012 Somalia Human Development Report*, Somalia has an estimated per capita income of US$284, the fourth worst in the world (UNDP 2012, 25). The economic and social costs of fragility in Somalia are substantial. Prolonged conflict and cyclical famine caused by recurrent drought and flood have displaced millions of people. According to the United Nations High Commission for Refugees (UNHCR), there are about 1 million Somali refugees in the region that have left Somalia, and 1.3 million remain internally displaced due to conflict and drought conditions (UNHCR 2013).

There may be disparate theories about how piracy developed in Somalia, but the accounts of the pirates-foot soldiers interviewed for this study indicate that poverty and lack of job opportunities was one of the main reasons for taking to the high seas to hijack ships (see also World Bank 2013, 45). The combination of fragility, poverty, and continuing conflict in a coastal state like Somalia provides an opportunity for piracy activity to occur as one way to overcome poverty and survive.

In this regard, and in so far as the fragile situation relates to the subject of piracy, the fragility in Somalia created the space for pirate financiers to engage in pirate activities and get support from land-based power brokers, and access to unregulated financial institutions as well as investment opportunities in other illicit activity that is often associated with violence.

Somali Piracy: A Gateway out of Poverty

Pirate financiers found an abundant workforce, since Somali piracy developed in coastal town areas where some fishermen were not able to make a living (Davey 2010). Nevertheless, it should be kept in mind that most of the first pirate financiers were neither desperate nor fishermen (Bahaduur 2011; Hansen 2012). After the complete collapse of the Somali government in 1991, including the subsequent collapse of the Somali navy and other coastal security authorities, the fishermen off the Somali coast could no longer be protected from foreign ships fishing in Somali waters. Illegal international fishing and maritime dumping went unchecked during the 1990s and probably continued thereafter (UN Security Council Report, October 2011, 11–13, paragraphs 40, 47, and 48; Greenpeace 2010), which in turn undermined the Somali coastal communities' economic prospects (New York Times 2008). As the institutions of Somalia broke down,

Somali fishermen had only themselves to look to for protection and became an easy target for pirate leaders and financiers willing to develop their activities and pirate networks (Hansen 2012). Holding vessels, cargo, and people as hostages became a lucrative business model, earning an estimated US$339 million to US$413 million in ransoms between April 2005 and December 2012 (UNODC-WB 2012).

In addition, over the last 20 years, Somalia has faced a devastating drought, which has led to one of the worst humanitarian disasters of the 20th century. The 2008 report by the UN International Expert Group on Piracy off the Somali Coast states the following regarding the overall state of affairs of Somalia and how a confluence of factors has resulted in the perfect opportunity for criminal groups of pirates to seize control:

> …poverty, lack of employment, environmental hardship, pitifully low incomes, reduction of pastoralist and maritime resources due to drought and illegal fishing and a volatile security and political situation all contribute to the rise and continuance of piracy in Somalia. (International Expert Group 2008, 15)

Even though piracy has to some extent been a way (albeit a misguided one) for some people to try and find an alternative to economic hardship and the impossibility of feeding their families, it has also played a role in exacerbating the instability and insecurity in Somalia.[2] The development of "pirate-centric societies," which are supported by local communities in concerned port cities and towns, is accompanied by the development of militias and competing criminal gangs. Pirate leaders and financiers gain power and access to economic resources thanks to the ransoms they receive, which influences the balance and organization of the concerned communities, further undermining efforts to establish a legitimate government.

In a team interview with pirates, how entire communities can sometimes get involved was explained as follows:

> When a ship is caught, the pirates call at the city. Everybody celebrates. When the ship comes at the port, a crew comes to secure it. Everything is written down, every food, drink, any kind of transaction. The final amount will be deducted from the ransom at the end. The investor pays. Some people don't get involved in piracy but make a lot of money simply by selling stuff to pirates. They make their money and they leave.

The economic impact of piracy has caused an increase in the cost of living within certain areas of Somalia, creating false market incentives and thus further widening the poverty gap. As one interviewee explained, "with piracy everything became more and more expensive…"

One example is the cost of khat. While khat is sold at about US$20 to US$50 per kilogram in the streets of coastal cities such as in Galkayo and Garacad, pirates will pay up to three times the normal market price, reaching US$100 per kilogram.[3]

Criminal Influence on the Economy

Pirates and their networks have used their illicit flows from piracy to influence the economy in certain parts of Somalia. Governmental structures and administrations are still challenged to effectively implement their authority across the whole territory of Somalia, resulting in an uneasy coexistence among a range of nonstate actors operating in the various regions of Somalia. Nonstate actors compete for control of parts of the national territory in order to extract rents from illegal activities, and compete to influence certain economic activities. Marginal governmental control allows piracy activities to flourish and the proceeds it generates to be moved freely in and out of Somalia.

The networks established and operated by criminal groups are adaptable and can quickly redirect their focus on new ventures. Thus, it is important to enhance the capacity of government institutions to enforce the law, disrupt these criminal networks, and prevent them from maintaining a monopoly on the use of force.

The issue of illicit financial flows from piracy and their high degree of mobility in the region are not so much a quantitative issue as a qualitative threat. In other words, the proceeds generated give enough economic leverage to criminal kingpins to engage in certain economic sectors and thus influence the legitimate economy. The harmful effects of illicit financial flows are mostly felt in the sense that they allow illegitimate actors to gain economic and often political influence within a country. The absence of widely and uniformly enforced due diligence processes and other Anti-Money Laundering and Combating the Financing of Terrorism (AML/CFT) internationally recognized standards in most economies affected by financial flows from piracy, creates concerns that pirate financiers and other criminal kingpins may gain access to key resources and decision-making positions in affected countries.

Somali Pirate Networks

The evolution of Somali piracy networks can be broken down into three periods: pre-2008, 2008 to the end of 2010, and 2010 to the present. These three periods can be roughly associated to (a) the development of piracy from an amateurs' business to an organized activity, (b) the development of new competitors in the pirate business, and (c) piracy involving organized networks with members operating in different countries (Hansen 2012).[4] Increased pressure from maritime forces at sea has forced pirates to move more often along the coast and to increase their relationships and cooperation with other pirate networks (UNODC 2011a). The different pirate networks and their geographic locations in Somalia were detailed as early as 2010 in the "Report of the Monitoring Group on Somalia pursuant to Security Council Resolution 1853" (United Nations 2010).[5] At that time, the Monitoring Group then identified three main networks.

The first network, referred to as the Hobyo-Xarardheere network (HHN), was set up in the areas of Xarardheere. This network was already active before

2008 under the leadership of Mohamed Hassan Abdi, also known as "Afweyne."[6] The network evolved between 2008 and 2010–11 under a more scattered leadership, allowing networks operating from Hobyo to gain more operational independence (UN 2011a). Hobyo became more and more important with the entry of militants from Hizb Ul Islam in Xarardheere in May 2010, which pushed some pirates to flee Xarardheere at that moment (BBC 2010). For this reason, the present analysis will differentiate between the Mogadishu-Xarardheere network[7] and the Hobyo network for the period after January 2011.

The second network identified by the Monitoring Group is also known as the Puntland Piracy network. Its main figures until 2008 were Abshir Boyah and Abdi Garaad (UN 2010). More recently (since 2011–12), other kingpins and warlords have emerged. The most infamous is Ciise Mohamoud Yusuf, also known as Ciise Yulux,[8] who is alleged to be engaged in other types of criminal activities.[9]

The third network identified by the Monitoring Group was the Eastern Sanaag network,[10] which launches operations from the coastal town of Laasqoray. This network was smaller than the two others and is no longer active. However, data concerning the anchorage location of vessels kidnapped since 2012 (UNODC-WB 2012), and recent research (Garowe Online 2012b) tend to increasingly associate what would remain of this network with parts of the Puntland Piracy network operating in Bari and north Garacad.

Map 3.1 shows the evolution of these networks.

The Somali Piracy Business Model

Over time, the Somali piracy business model has become more sophisticated and has come to involve a number of investors, financiers, and other shareholders within Somalia, across the region, and even internationally.

The World Bank Report on the economic aspects of piracy offers a "reduced" business model of pirate operations.

The approach taken by our study adds a different angle, since the analysis focuses on other aspects. As explained in this study, the various networks operating have their own historical developments and are ever-evolving "organizations." The analysis developed in the coming chapter highlights three dominant models of financing an operation and sharing the proceeds—which one could call "business models"[11] for ease of reference. This study will differentiate and develop (a) the "artisanal" scheme, (b) the "cooperative" scheme, and (c) the individualistic scheme.[12]

The artisanal scheme concerns a limited number of low-level operations and a few relatives pooling their resources. The cooperative scheme is probably the most widespread and gathers several financiers (from three to five or sometimes more) who will invest in an operation in the form of shares. Investors partaking in this kind of operation will be rewarded proportionally to their original investment. It is the most "business-oriented" model, and the object of the World Bank report on the economic aspects of piracy (Do et al. 2013). After a ransom is paid,

Map 3.1 Evolution of the Main Pirate Networks until Today

Source: © United Nations. Used with permission; further permission required for re-use.
Note: The boundaries and names shown and the designations used on this map do not imply official endorsement or acceptance by the United Nations. Dashed lines represent undetermined boundaries. The final boundary between the Republic of Sudan and the Republic of South Sudan has not yet been determined.

all costs are paid and pirates receive their share (usually between US$30,000 and US$75,000), and financiers receive between 25 and 30 percent of the total ransom payment to share among themselves. The individualistic scheme is only accessible to financiers with sufficient financial capacity to sponsor an operation on their own. Consequently, the financier will control the operation and receive between 50 and 75 percent of the final ransom payment for himself.

The following statement captures how the "business of piracy" has evolved over time and gives an indication of the number of different parties that can be involved in the process:

> This business gives money to a lot of people. It involves lawyers on both sides, [i.e., on the side of pirates and the side of ship owners], consultants, security companies, shipping companies and businesses also supplying this whole world with food, oil, water and so on… Along the years, the activity became more and more professional. Deals that were sealed by word-of-mouth at the beginning now involve contracts. The trust is now based on money. For instance, a security company that will need contacts inside Somalia used to negotiate with elders who would facilitate their access in exchange of goods for their community. Now that lawyers entered the game, there is no in-kind contribution. First you sign a contract and deposit money in a bank account. Even the final ransom agreement is signed. The paper is signed on the side of pirates and that of the ship owner.
>
> On the side of pirates, many people are also involved. Amongst the team that comes to guard the ship on shore, you will find even girls. The money is not just counted once delivered, it is examined by people who have the skills for it. It's not just the pirates that count it, but people who come on board and have professional machines to detect fake money. It takes a while to count US$2 or 3 million in cash. The translator who negotiates is also brought on board. Some of them are well known and have assisted in more than 20 negotiations. Some come before the negotiations to assess the ship in order to calibrate the ransom demand.[13]

When questioned about how the piracy business model operates, pirates interviewed for the study advised the team that businessmen that operate on the coast make significant profits by supporting piracy operations by selling goods to the pirates. The cost of every commodity sold to the pirates—food, fuel, khat, alcohol, and so forth—has at least tripled.[14] All pirates accept the situation and realize this is the cost and social norm of doing business. Concerning transferring or changing money (U.S. dollars to Somali shillings), they were of the opinion that there were no real constraints.[15]

Somali Piracy: Problems and Responses

Regional Instability

Piracy has a destabilizing effect on Somalia and constitutes a significant threat to regional stability. It also leads to an increase in prices, insecurity of energy supplies, and loss of revenue throughout the region.[16]

The waters surrounding the Horn of Africa are recognized as some of the most dangerous in the world. This has resulted in the decline of fishing in these waters; compared to other regions in the world, exports of fish products from piracy-affected countries have declined by 28.5 percent since 2006. There has also been a significant decrease in tourism in East African countries such as Kenya, and in islands in the Indian Ocean, such as Mauritius and the Seychelles. Reports suggest that tourism expenditures in East Africa were 25 percent lower than in Sub-Saharan African countries as a result of growing fears stemming from the increasing incidence of tourists being taken hostage by pirates, terrorism, and kidnappings for other reasons (Do et al. 2013; Mubarak 2011).

A Global Problem

Not only does piracy create problems in the region, but it also creates global problems. In a world where currently 80 percent of international trade is conducted by sea, unchallenged piracy is not only a menace to political stability and a threat to international security, but it also undermines global growth prospects going forward. According to the World Bank Report, Somali piracy has cost a yearly average of US$18 billion loss to world trade. It is the assessment of the World Bank Report that Piracy has had the same effect as imposing an additional 1.1 percent value-added tax on all shipments that transit through the waters affected by Somali pirate activities. Insurance premiums for cargo, crew, and vessels that sail in these waters have increased, as has the cost of rerouting or canceling shipments.[17] Ships have also had to use enhanced security measures, Best Management Practices, and have increasingly contracted armed security firms to counter pirate attacks.[18]

Global Efforts against Pirates

As part of a global response to the piracy problem, the international community has made significant efforts to mobilize counter piracy operations. It is the responsibility of the International Maritime Bureau Piracy Reporting Centre (IMB PRC) at the International Chamber of Commerce to monitor and collect data on piracy attacks around the world.

The international response to the problem has essentially been a top-down approach mainly under the mandate of United Nations Security Council resolutions allowing engagement by law enforcement, intelligence agencies, and military assets from NATO (the North Atlantic Treaty Organization); the European Union through the European Union Naval Force Somalia (EUNAVFOR), the United States, and others.[19]

The Contact Group on Piracy off the Coast of Somalia (CGPCS), a voluntary international forum created in January 2009 pursuant to UN Security Council Resolution 1851, has been at the forefront in leading the international community's[20] response to piracy by facilitating discussion and coordinating actions among states and organizations to suppress piracy off the coast of Somalia.

The CGPCS has made progress on many fronts including coordinating naval patrols, establishing a trust fund to assist prosecutions, addressing legal deficiencies in piracy-related laws, promoting shipping Best Management Practices, and developing a strategic communications plan. The CGPCS created "Working Group 5" during its 9th Plenary Session in July 2011, with a mandate to coordinate international efforts to identify and disrupt the financial networks of pirate leaders and their financiers, in recognition of the fact that the successful eradication of piracy is possible only if the illicit funding including the financial gains from piracy and financial flows related to piracy are dismantled.

While the focus has been on naval operations to combat piracy, this study proposes that interventions focused to stop the financial flows from proceeds of piracy are just as important in dealing with the problem.

The next chapters discuss the financial flows from piracy activities off the Horn of Africa. How much money is being made and what happens to these proceeds of piracy, in particular how are they moved and reinvested?

Notes

1. According to the World Bank, "Fragile Situations" have either (a) a harmonized average CPIA country rating of 3.2 or less, or (b) the presence of a UN and/or regional peace-keeping or peace-building mission during the past three years. The World Bank's CPIA is done annually for all its borrowing countries. It has evolved into a set of criteria, which are grouped in four clusters: (a) economic management, (b) structural policies, (c) policies for social inclusion and equity, and (d) public sector management and institutions. The number of criteria, currently 16, reflects a balance between ensuring that all key factors that foster propoor growth and poverty alleviation are captured, without overly burdening the evaluation process. Ratings for each of the criteria reflect a variety of indicators, observations, and judgments. They focus on the quality of each country's current policies and institutions, which are the main determinant of current aid effectiveness prospects.

2. In 2008, the United Nations Security Council, recognizing the seriousness of the threat posed by Somali piracy, passed Resolution 1816, which states that piracy "exacerbate[s] the situation in Somalia[,] which continues to constitute a threat to international peace and security in the region."

3. This will be discussed in greater detail in chapter 8. See also UN (2011a), which supports the team's findings, suggesting that pirates may pay up to US$150 per kilogram for khat.

4. Even though Hansen separates the period pre-2006 and 2006–08 as a reconfiguration period, for the sake of clarity, it was decided to combine these two periods, especially since the predominant actors of the piracy business and the geographic areas affected by pirate operations inside Somalia remained mostly the same until 2008. (See also UNODC 2011a.)

5. Presented to the United Nations Security Council by letter dated February 26, 2010.

6. Afweyne is a nickname meaning "big mouth." (See UN 2010; Hansen 2012.)

7. This network is broadly associated to followers of Afweyne and his son.

8. Also known as Isse Mohamoud Yusuf, Isse Yuluh, Isse Yulux, Esse Yuluh, Esse Yulux, Issa Yuhluw.

9. See Case Study in chapter 7.

10. Report of the Monitoring Group on Somalia pursuant to Security Council Resolution 1853 2008).
11. In 2011, the Financial Action Task Force identified three methods used to finance a pirate operation: (a) a "cottage"-type of investment with only one financier, (b) a "shareholder"-type of investment where pirates going to sea are their own investors, and (c) a "syndicate"-type of investment, where financiers collectively finance an operation. This scheme may be analytically slightly outdated now since the "cottage" type could more efficiently be associated to major pirate financiers who have already gained a lot of money from piracy and are now organizing large-scale operations, far from the small-scale operations organized via that type of investment in the early days. The "shareholder" type is reported further in this study, under section II, chapter 5 as the "Artisanal cooperative," and the "syndicate" type is similar to the "Hobyo-Xarardheere" cooperative scheme discussed in that same chapter.
12. See chapter 5 for a more detailed presentation.
13. Interview with Andrew Mwangura, Director of the East African Seafarers' Association Programme, October 13, 2011.
14. See chapter 5 for more details.
15. The only restriction is that some Somali Money or Value Transfer Services do not accept transactions over US$1,000. If a transaction is over US$1,000, they usually conduct several individual transactions. They also move funds within Somalia via mobile banking. See chapter 6 for more details.
16. See the Contact Group on Piracy website at http://www.thecgpcs.org/about.do?action=background.
17. Interview with Djibouti Chamber of Commerce, Director of Djibouti Customs, and Port of Djibouti officials, June 2–3, 2012; interview with Ethiopian Insurance Corporation and Awash Insurance Company June 11, 2012.
18. See Best Management Practices published by the International Maritime Organization in order to prevent piracy and armed robbery against ships off the coast of Somalia, and its Interim Guidance to Private Companies Providing Privately Contracted Armed Security Personnel On Board Ships in the High Risk Area; http://www.imo.org/MediaCentre/HotTopics/piracy/Documents/1339.pdf; http://www.imo.org/OurWork/Security/SecDocs/Documents/Piracy/MSC.1-Circ.1443.pdf.
19. Warships under the national commands of China, India, Iran, Japan, the Russian Federation, and Saudi Arabia have also been patrolling the seas for pirates.
20. The CGPCS has bought together more than 60 countries and international organizations in the fight against piracy (http://www.thecgpcs.org).

SECTION II

Understanding the Financial Flows

Figure II.1 Following the Money

Chapter 4: Ransoms
Starting point: Ransom negotiations
How much money are we talking about?

↓

Chapter 5: Distributing the Proceeds
To whom are the monies distributed once the ransom payment has been received?

1. **Low-Level Pirates—"Foot Soldiers"**
   What do they typically spend their wages on?
2. **Local Communities**
   What local services are provided to the pirates?
3. **Financiers**
   How much do they receive?
   Understanding the investment schemes for a piracy business model

↓

Chapter 6: How Are the Proceeds Moved?

1. **Financial wire transfers**
2. **Trade-based money laundering**
3. **Money or value transfer services (MVTS)**
4. **Cross-border cash smuggling**

↓

Chapter 7: How Do Pirate Financiers Invest Their Proceeds?
Investing in legitimate business activities
and investing in criminal activities

↓

Focus Chapter 8: Khat and Real Estate
Investing in khat and
real estate

Pirate Trails • http://dx.doi.org/10.1596/978-0-8213-9963-7

CHAPTER 4

Ransoms

Starting Point: Law Firms Negotiating Ransoms

Such is the threat of piracy that the Joint War Committee of Insurers in London has declared the waters off the coast of Somalia a war zone.[1] Ships operating in the region are encouraged to take out insurance against acts of piracy. The peril of piracy can be insured either in the traditional Hull and Machinery insurance policy or in a more specialized War Risk policy, depending on the vessel owner's insurance plan (Jardine Lloyd Thompson Ltd 2009). Depending on which approach is taken (Hull and Machinery, or War Risk), the peril of piracy can be insured using different limits of coverage and different deductibles. Another insurance option available to the vessel owner is to purchase a separate insurance policy for the release of the crew, a policy called Kidnapping and Ransom. This policy is often used when the vessel owner wants high limits for ransom payments or finds the premium being charged for the piracy peril is too high in traditional Hull and Machinery or War Risk coverage. Some law firms specialize in assisting vessel owners in assessing the optimal type of insurance coverage for their needs. In following the money, the team decided to discover what happens from the moment a ship is hijacked and a ransom is demanded.

In January 2012, members of the team met with law firms operating from London that were identified as leaders in the provision of advice regarding piracy matters such as K&R response services. The team explained the project and advised the law firms that the focus of the study was to trace the illicit flows from piracy and that information they have might assist the team in better determining how much money was actually paid in ransom payments and the methodology on how ransom payments are executed. These law firms can become involved within 30 minutes of a hijacking. The services they provide include (a) liaising with the family of the crew, (b) providing advice on legality and potential sanctions associated with ransom payments, (c) conducting negotiations (some law firms were more actively involved in ransom negotiations than others), (d) supporting operational matters for the actual payment of ransoms, and (e) advising on insurance disputes and coverage issues.

When a ransom is negotiated by law firms, the companies interviewed by the team said that, most of the time, the discussion about ransom payments was controlled by the ship owner. In terms of compliance, the team was informed that, for each case of ransom payment, financial institutions contacted for cash withdrawal were made aware that the cash would serve as a ransom payment. With regard to risks associated with potential terrorist financing, the law firms employ internal and external diligence resources in each case, and liaise with the appropriate intelligence agencies in order to determine instances where the payment of a ransom should not proceed.

The law firms stated that their knowledge of the money's destination was limited. The law firms mentioned having no recollection of a case where they paid a ransom through a wire transfer, or where an offshore financial center would be used to route the monies for ransom payment. They also assert that they have no knowledge of ransom monies used to directly pay lawyers or professional advisers.

The law firms also defended their work under the argument of the Right to Life principle under the U.K. Human Rights Act. With respect to the possibility of legal challenge under the U.K. Proceeds of Crime Act, the law firms contended that the money involved in the payment of ransoms did not ultimately become proceeds of crime. While some of the law firms routinely submitted suspicious activity reports (SARs) to the Serious Organized Crime Agency, the majority did not, and were of the opinion that they had no obligation to do so.

Conscious of their duties regarding client confidentiality, the firms were guarded in their comments. They expressed a degree of skepticism about the project, voicing the concerns of their clients who feel that too many demands have been made on them to provide information, but little is done to help them. The firms reported that ship owners, in particular, were apprehensive about the sanctioning in 2010 of two Somali pirate financiers/leaders by the Office of Foreign Assets Control (OFAC). They are concerned that the sanctions could prevent the payment of a ransom and that the United States and possibly others may choose to go beyond sanctioning pirates and ban ransom payments. Where ransom payments have come to be seen by some ship owners, as a "cost of doing business," they believed that such action to ban ransom payments would interfere with their interests. Logically, the next question is: So how much money are Somali pirates earning from this "business"?

How Much Money Are We Talking About?

Between 2005 and December 2012,[2] the UNODC-WB dataset estimates that between US$339 million and US$413 million was paid in the form of ransoms for ships and/or seafarers kidnapped by Somali pirates. A number of fishing vessels or small dhows hijacked between 2005 and 2012 end up "disappearing" from the joint dataset. Indeed, while being accounted for as successfully hijacked, and showing no report of release, these vessels are no longer accounted for off the Somali coast. It is the team's assumption that these vessels have eventually been

Figure 4.1 Ships Successfully Hijacked

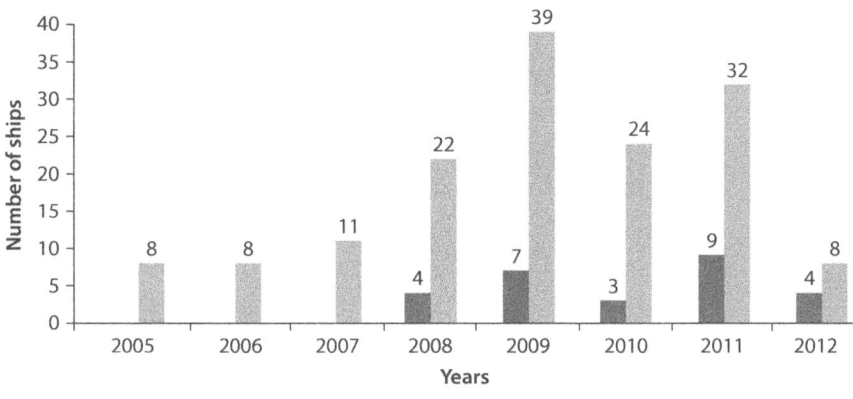

Source: UNODC-WB 2012.

turned into mother ships and are either still operational at sea under pirate command or have been sunk or otherwise been neutralized (being seized by military forces or coast guards, for instance) in the course of their operations under pirate command. However, the number of ships still being used as mother ships is very limited, and no fishing vessels were being held at anchorage by Somali pirates at the time of finalizing this study. Therefore, the persistence of these cases in the joint dataset should also be attributed to gaps in the reporting. In addition, a number of vessels are released without a ransom for various reasons, such as the intervention of military forces, or negotiations leading to other compensations to pirates. However, the vast majority of vessels hijacked and released by pirates between 2008 and 2012 ended up being ransomed (see figure 4.1).

Figure 4.2 sums up the evolution of ransoms collected by pirates per year, showing both low and high estimates.

The most lucrative year for pirates was 2011, when they collected between US$151.1 million and US$155.67 million. However, the real shift in amounts collected occurred between 2007 and 2009, when the number of ships released against a ransom payment more than tripled within 24 months. Although only 22 ships were released after payment of a ransom in 2008, 42 were hijacked that year, leaving pirates with a considerable number of ships to be released the following year or to be used as mother ships (see figure 4.4).

Ultimately, the data reflect that 2008–09 is when pirates started to capture ships faster than they would release them. This was due to pirates' increased success at sea, but also to the fact that negotiations for the release of vessels started to become increasingly lengthy, sometimes taking more than a year (UNODC-WB 2012). As in any business, increased stocks imply higher operating costs. In this case, more ships captured and held imply, among other things, more hostages to guard and feed, and more militias on shore (needed to guard the crews and vessels), all of whom need to be paid and fed. In 2009, 46 vessels were released

Figure 4.2 Evolution of Ransoms: Annual Amounts Collected by Somali Pirates in Ransom for Vessels and/or Crews Kidnapped between 2005 and 2012

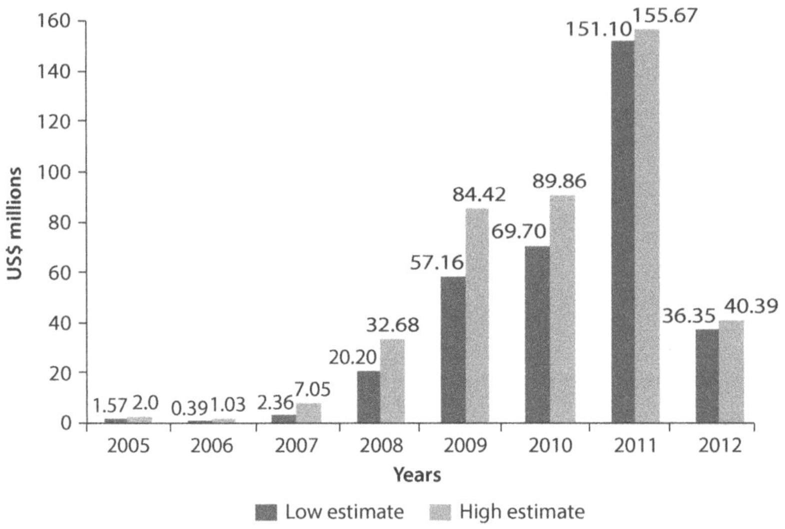

Source: UNODC-WB 2012.

after a ransom was paid (compared to 26 in 2008 and 27 in 2010), which can be viewed as an attempt to lower costs induced by an increased stock of vessels (the equivalent of a business reducing inventory).

In 2010, pirates released only 24 vessels against a ransom of 50 captured. The higher overall amount collected in ransom monies despite fewer ransoms paid is attributed, in this case, to an increase in average ransom payments, which rose from an estimated US$2.2 million in 2009 to an estimated US$3.67 million in 2010. But in 2011, pirates collected their largest amount of ransoms (estimated between US$151.1 million and US$155.67 million for that year), preceding a year that would be the least successful in terms of total annual payment since 2007. Beyond the success imputed to navies patrolling the waters and the increased presence of armed guards aboard vessels, the following analysis shows that the results of 2011 and 2012 can also be understood by considering the "stocks" of hijacked vessels amassed by Somali pirates at the end of each year. This increase in supply helps to forecast why 2012 and 2013 do not represent the final years of Somali piracy (figure 4.3).

Explaining the "Peak" of 2011 and the Decrease in 2012

As explained above, between 2008 and the end of 2010, Somali pirates captured more vessels than they would release for ransom. In 2010, pirates released 24 vessels for ransom while they still held 28 vessels captive at the end of that same year.[3] In other words, their stocks at the beginning of 2011 were already bigger than the number of ships they released in 2010. It was therefore almost certain, at the beginning of 2011, that pirates' proceeds would be higher in 2011 than in

Figure 4.3 Average Amount of Ransom Payments

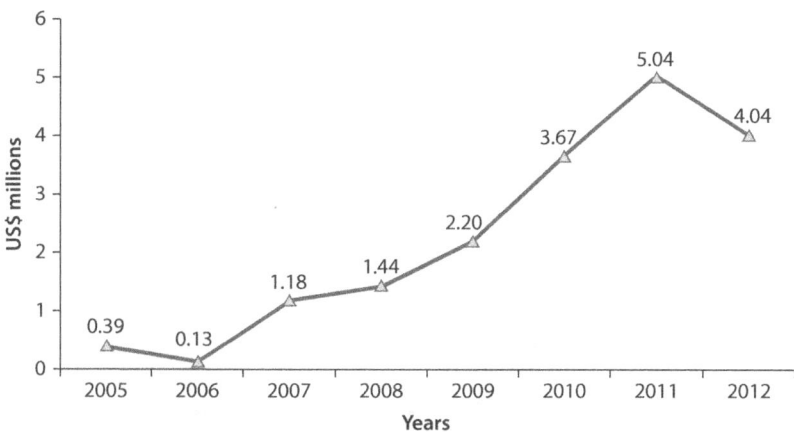

Source: UNODC-WB 2012.

2010, should the average amount of ransom payments remain the same, and should pirates be able to obtain a ransom for all the ships they still held captive. Ransom amounts not only failed to drop, but they skyrocketed to a record average payment of US$5.04 million per ransom. As a result, despite less success at sea in 2011 than in 2010, proceeds collected by pirates in 2011 reached a peak estimated at US$151.1 million to US$155.67 million.

Due to the increased presence of private security personnel aboard vessels transiting through piracy-affected areas, coupled with the action of military flotillas in the region, the number of successful hijackings started to decrease in 2011. For the first time since 2008, pirates released more ships for ransom in 2011 than they captured that year. At the end of 2011, the number of ships held at anchorage by Somali pirates was down to 7 compared to 28 at the end of 2010. In 2012, Somali pirates were able to successfully hijack 15 vessels compared to 48 in 2009, 50 in 2010, and 31 in 2011. Figure 4.4 illustrates the decline in ransoms paid since 2010.

Average ransom payments in 2012 are estimated at over US$4 million per ransom. Pirates also captured more vessels in 2012 than they released for ransom. At the end of 2012, there were only four ships being held at anchorage by Somali pirates (EUNAVFOR 2013). However, the ransoms paid for both ships released at the beginning of 2013 reportedly totaled US$13 million, suggesting that the remaining ships will likely collect higher ransoms per ships than in 2012, if they manage to capture more ships. Furthermore, considering the amounts already collected by pirate financiers until the end of 2012, pirates' capacities to conduct operations are probably far from declining. In that sense, the declining activity of pirates at sea may well be only a temporary break.

With so much money being raised, the inevitable question is what happens to these monies? How are they distributed and moved inside and outside of Somalia?

Figure 4.4 Stocks and Flows of Ships Held and Released

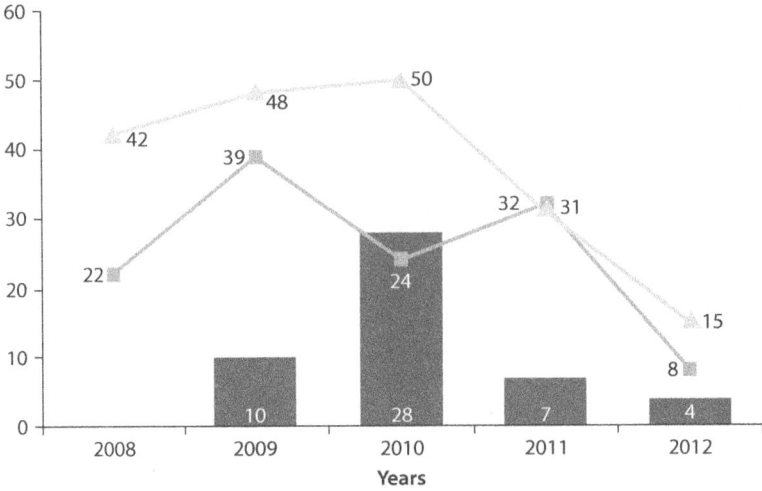

Stock—number of ships held at anchorage in Somalia at the end of a given year
Number of ships released for ransom
Number of successful hijackings

Sources: UNODC-WB 2012, EUNAVFOR.

Notes

1. http://www.lmalloyds.com/Web/market_places/marine/JWC/Joint_War.aspx.
2. The present study uses a version of the dataset including ransom payments until December 2012, which is a longer time coverage than that used in the World Bank report (Do et al. 2013), thus explaining differences in figures used.
3. Interview with EUNAVFOR analyst in Seychelles on 7 March 2013.

CHAPTER 5

Distributing the Proceeds

Low-Level Pirates—"Foot Soldiers"

Once a vessel is hijacked by a pirate action group (PAG), it is brought to the shore where the negotiator (also called the "interpreter") assesses the value of the ship. Sometimes a second person accompanies the negotiator, specifically to assess the value of the ship. Reportedly, interpreters get paid US$10,000 to US$20,000.

When a ransom is received, it is payday for the low-level pirates who were sent out to sea to hijack the concerned vessel(s). Members of the PAG get paid US$30,000 to US$75,000, (which amounts to about 0.01 percent to 0.025 percent of an average ransom payment). This is a standard fee agreed to before the piracy operation. There is a bonus for the first pirate to board the hijacked ship and for those bringing their own weapon or ladder, which can be up to an additional US$10,000[1] (UNODC 2011a).

The most commonly reported expenses of low-level pirates are for sex workers or slaves and trafficked girls,[2] khat, alcohol, and expensive cars.[3] During an interview by the team with members of the Youth Organization Against Piracy in Garowe, Puntland, one of the reformed pirates acknowledged that he had been involved in a hijacking that successfully collected a US$2.5 million ransom. His investor received approximately US$800,000 and he received US$40,000. Of the US$40,000 he spent US$10,000 on a car and loaned US$20,000 to a friend who wanted to reinvest in another operation that ultimately failed. The remaining US$10,000 was spent on "leisure" in Garowe, he said. The rest of the interviewees present during that interview further confirmed that the vast majority of the money was spent on leisure. Several interviews led by the team during field research confirmed that the alcohol used by pirates came from Ethiopia; the khat from Kenya; and sex workers and trafficked girls from Djibouti, Ethiopia, and Somaliland.

Khat is often provided to pirate foot soldiers on credit during the operation. Their consumption is recorded in books and, when the ransom is dropped, a pirate gets paid his share, minus the equivalent of what he consumed on credit.[4]

Other costs deducted from payments include food[5] and fines imposed for bad behavior. It is not known how widespread these rules concerning bad behavior are among networks, but their use was reported to the team by the Commander of the European Union Naval Force,[6] and was mentioned in a document prepared for the 2011 UNODC Conference on Illicit Financial Flows Linked to Piracy (UNODC 2011a). The fines listed in the document include mistreating the crew (a US$5,000 fine and dismissal), refusal to follow an order (a US$10,000 fine and dismissal), and falling asleep on post (a US$5,000 fine) (UNODC 2011a). This system is one of the reasons why most pirates find it difficult to retire after their first expedition; they often contract so much debt that they are left with almost nothing after they are done reimbursing their expenses.[7]

This type of spending on leisure and line of credit are some of the main reasons why most foot soldiers eventually go back to sea.[8] This behavior can be associated with a general feeling of loss, and the low education level of the vast majority of foot soldiers.[9] Acknowledging the lack of figures to guide their behavior, a convicted pirate, interviewed by the team in Shimo La Tewa prison in Mombasa on August 7, 2012, concluded the discussion with the following statement:

> If I go back to Somalia, I would like to pursue an education. Because right now I don't know what is right and what is wrong. In Somalia people are born Muslim and they know how to recite the Qur'an. But everybody forgot what the actual principles are.

The assessment of pirate financiers' expenses and proceeds (see chapter 7) only marginally takes into account these expenses on leisure. The assumption is made that financiers are more educated, because they need to speak English in order to follow negotiations, or even reportedly have capacities in terms of providing financial services (see chapter 7); and that their expenses on leisure, even if they represent the same amounts as for foot soldiers, proportionally represent only a fraction of the financiers' proceeds.

Monies Flowing to Local Communities

On shore, another militia, distinct from the PAG, guards the vessel, and a complete economy comes to life to support the captured ship (UNODC 2011a). Cooks provide catering services for the crew and pirates. Khat is brought on shore, and many other services, including alcohol and prostitution, are provided.[10]

The khat supplier, cooks, and other businessmen (in the sense of local private entrepreneurs) providing these services to the "pirate community" get reimbursed once the ransom is paid.[11] Each service provided is recorded and receipts are kept by the businessmen.[12] Goods or services are loaned at up to 100 percent interest for pirates.[13] For instance, if a pirate requests US$10 of airtime for his cell phone, and promises to pay once he receives the money from an upcoming ransom, he will have to pay back not US$10, but US$20, to the shopkeeper who provided him with airtime. As explained during interviews with pirates in custody,

When the ship comes at the port, a crew comes to secure it. Everything is written down, every food, drink, any kind of transaction. The final amount will be deducted from the ransom at the end [i.e., the payment that a pirate will receive once the ransom is paid]. The investor pays [what pirates owe to local businessmen]. Some people don't get involved in piracy but make a lot of money simply by selling stuff to pirates. They make their money and they leave ... A bookkeeper gets to each guy owing money and collects the money once [the ransom] is paid.

In some cases, payments are also made to local militias controlling a port, such as the agreement that was set with Al-Shabaab in Xarardheere, whereby pirates would share 20 percent of their ransom payments with the militia (Ahmed and Sheikh 2011; Do et al. 2013; United Nations 2011a).

The Lions' Share: How Do Financiers Invest and Benefit from Piracy?

Financiers reportedly receive 30 percent up to 75 percent of the ransom payment,[14] depending on their initial investment. However, the most commonly accepted figure is 30 percent of the total ransom payment going to financiers (UN 2011a, S/2011/433; UNODC 2011a).

While a certain modus operandi is assigned to each scheme, in reality, the methods of financing, sharing ransoms, and moving money are fluid and overlap among the different schemes, and these networks and modus operandi are ever evolving. However, the three networks presented at the beginning of this report[15] and the three periods of time of their operations will serve as an analytical framework particularly when the analysis focuses on the evolution of financiers' investments and tactics over time. It is important to emphasize the need to analyze this issue and related networks as an ever evolving structure.

The Artisanal Scheme

Not all pirate operations are part of a wider syndicate. For instance, some "amateur" pirates have been seen operating in the Gulf of Aden (UNODC 2011a). It is not known what proportion of pirate activities are being sponsored in this way. These operations are of a lower scale and are mainly composed of members of the same family or relatives who share the cost of preparing the operation, either by bringing money or instruments, such as weapons, or a ladder, for instance (Hansen 2012; UNODC 2011a). The cost of such an operation is estimated to be no more than US$300 (Hansen 2012), and its success rather limited. The return on investment is proportionate to the original investment, based on the ransom received and after all costs have been deducted.

The Cooperative Scheme

The "Report of the Monitoring Group on Somalia and Eritrea pursuant to Security Council Resolution 1916" (United Nations 2011)[16] highlights the "shareholder" model of the financing of piracy, and confirmed the initial findings presented by the UNODC for the first UNODC Conference on Illicit Financial Flows Linked to Piracy off the coast of Somalia, held in Nairobi, May 17–19, 2011.

This model can also be considered a natural development of the artisanal cooperative-type model. A committee of financiers is formed to collect enough money to sponsor a pirate expedition (Jorisch 2011). Pirate expeditions involving cartels and two skiffs[17] cost an average of US$30,000 (Hansen 2012). Several financiers might finance an operation, each contributing US$5,000 to US$10,000 (UNODC 2011a). The money collected is given to the pirate leader, who will be in charge of organizing the expedition; recruiting members of the PAG; and obtaining weapons, fuel, khat, food, and water required for the expedition (Hansen 2012). The PAG always includes at least one team member who can speak some English and who can read a ship manifesto—typically the pirate leader.[18] A second leader, who commands the force on shore and is in charge of securing the pirate base and captured vessels, is also part of the committee of financiers setting up an operation (UN 2011a S/2011/433).

The Individualistic Scheme

Reporting indicates that some financiers can receive as much as 50 percent to 75 percent from a ransom payment (UNODC 2012). This suggests that the concerned financiers were the sole investors for those specific acts of piracy. Sole investors have been shown to collect between 50 percent (for instance, the MV Blue Star released in March 2009 and the MV Al Nisr Al Saud released in July 2010) and 75 percent of the total ransom (in the case of the MV Thor Star released in May 2009, for instance) (UNODC 2012). This strategy allows the financier to maintain a higher degree of control over the whole operation, meaning that the militias at sea and on land answer to the same commander.

How to Get the Cash inside Somalia to Prepare an Operation

Reportedly, some financiers have only limited amounts of cash inside Somalia but substantial deposits in banks abroad.[19] To overcome this problem when financing a pirate operation, financiers act as import/export facilitators—one could associate this process to "reversed trade-based money-laundering." For instance, a pirate financier will associate with a legitimate businessman operating inside Somalia who needs to purchase goods or supplies in a country B (see figure 5.1). The financier will ask his counterpart Y in country B to purchase the goods or supplies required by the legitimate businessman, using the pirate financiers' money located in his bank account abroad. These goods or supplies are then shipped to the businessman inside Somalia. Upon receipt, the businessman repays the financiers in cash for the value of the shipment and goods or supplies that were shipped to Somalia for him. The operation incurred no transfer costs for the financier, who can then use the cash received from the businessman to pay for his criminal operations.

Figure 5.1 False Invoicing to Finance Pirate Operations

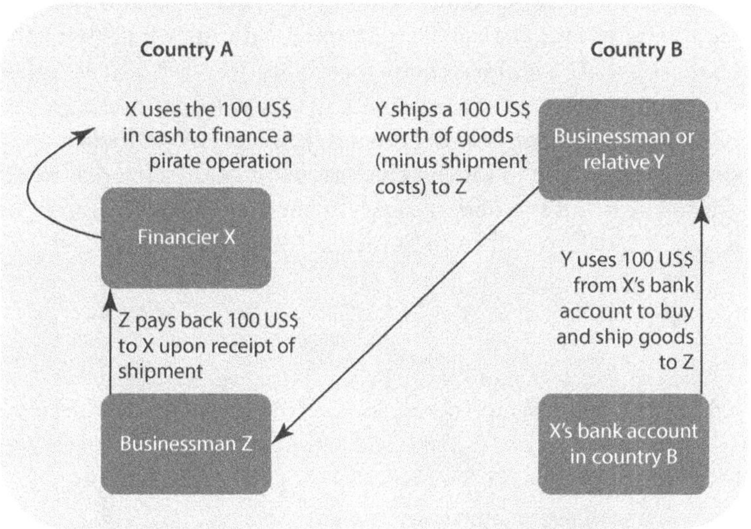

```
Country A                              Country B

X uses the 100 US$      Y ships a 100 US$
in cash to finance a    worth of goods        Businessman or
pirate operation        (minus shipment       relative Y
                        costs) to Z

   Financier X
                                        Y uses 100 US$
                                        from X's bank
Z pays back 100 US$                     account to buy
to X upon receipt of                    and ship goods
shipment                                to Z

   Businessman Z                        X's bank account
                                        in country B
```

Source: Formulation based on discussions with the Seychelles Financial Intelligence Unit.
Note: The amounts used are for demonstration purposes only and do not represent actual amounts.

Financiers Abroad

While investigating the case of the MV Pompei, hijacked on April 18, 2012, the Belgian authorities discovered that the pirate negotiator had ties to Dubai, in the United Arab Emirates, and located bank accounts and identification numbers in that country (FATF 2011). In addition, Belgian authorities estimate that, following the ransom drop, the money was taken to Djibouti where it was sent via Money or Value Transfer Services to Dubai (FATF 2011). This case clearly shows the links between pirates in Somalia and the ultimate destination of the money abroad.

Other financial wire transfers linking pirates with counterparts abroad have been identified. In its 2012 report, the United Nations Monitoring Group on Somalia and Eritrea stated that:

> Investigating the movements and the investments of piracy proceeds, the Monitoring Group has identified several financial transfers between Somali pirates and individuals in the Somali diaspora, linked to a number of hijacking cases such as the MV Al Khaliq (2009), MV Orna (2010), MV Irene SL (2011), Zirku (2011), MV Rosalio D'Amato (2011) and MV Enrico Ievoli (2011). (United Nations 2012a)

Investigations of pirate chiefs and financiers concern countries in North America (AP 2011), Africa, Asia, and Europe.[20] Reportedly, bank accounts located outside of Somalia and holding proceeds from piracy have been identified by law enforcement agencies during investigations related to cases of maritime piracy and related kidnapping for ransom off the coast of Somalia.[21]

Pirate financiers and investors constitute a vast network, mainly operating on land. In Somalia, that network has gained considerable economic and political capacities. This double grip on Somali society, coupled with their links with the diaspora[22] and their assets abroad, give them the ability to reach out to other capacities when their operations at sea become less successful, as has been the case since 2012. Therefore, the question is: How do financiers move their money within and outside Somalia? The following chapter analyzes the channels available to and used by pirates and the underground financial circuit that allows for illicit financial flows to transit to and from Somalia.

Notes

1. Several reports on the exact amounts exist in the literature. A bracket between US$10,000 and US$75,000 seems to encompass all the different options, including potential bonuses.
2. See case studies in appendix A on human trafficking for piracy.
3. Interviews of the team with pirate inmates and reformed pirates.
4. Interviews of the team with pirates in custody in the Seychelles.
5. Interviews of the team with pirate inmates and reformed pirates.
6. Interview with Rear-Admiral Jean-Baptise Dupuis, then Commander of the European Union Naval Force, Djibouti, June 3, 2012.
7. Interviews of the team with pirates in custody in the Seychelles.
8. Interviews of the team with pirate inmates and reformed pirates.
9. UNODC interview with Andrew Mwangura, Director of the East African Seafarers' Association Programme, October 13, 2011.
10. Interviews of the team with pirate inmates and reformed pirates.
11. Interviews of the team with pirates in custody in the Seychelles.
12. Correspondence with the Seychelles' Financial Intelligence Unit, December 2, 2012.
13. Interviews with pirates in custody.
14. For an explanation of shares amounting to 50 percent of the total ransom and above, see section below.
15. See analysis in chapter 3 in section on Somali Pirate Networks.
16. Presented to the United Nations Security Council by letter dated June 20, 2011.
17. As defined in the Concise Oxford English Dictionary (Oxford University 2008), a skiff is a light rowing boat or sculling boat, typically for one person.
18. Interviews with the Youth Organization Against Piracy, in Garowe, Puntland, April 2012.
19. Correspondence with the Seychelles' Financial Intelligence Unit, December 2, 2012.
20. Correspondence with the Seychelles' Financial Intelligence Unit, December 2, 2012.
21. INTERPOL, Global Database on Piracy
22. For more elements on these links, please refer to the coming chapters, especially on financial transfers, trade-based money laundering, and other investments in legitimate activities.

CHAPTER 6

How Are the Proceeds Moved?

There is no real constraint in moving the money or changing it. The only restriction is that hawalas do not accept transactions over US$1,000. Rather, they will ask to divide the operation in several transactions and use mobile banking.[1]

Financial Wire Transfers

The access to financial wire transfers from Somalia is permitted by financial routes that facilitate Somali businessmen's operations despite the ongoing instability in Somalia and the collapse of the state infrastructures (Nenova 2005). Djibouti and Dubai have become the main transit points for business operations related to Somalia.[2] Moreover, Dubai has also become a key trading partner for Somalia given its advantage in logistics and services it provides to businesses operating from Dubai.

The Somali economy is mainly based on livestock trade with the Gulf States (Majid 2010), which is why most transactions go to Dubai, in the United Arab Emirates.[3] Most businessmen involved in that trade have based their activities in Dubai.[4] Initially, funds from those businesses would transit through Djibouti via Letters of Credit.[5] Now that businessmen have based most of their operations in Dubai, transfers often go from the importer's bank account in a Dubai-based financial institution, to the exporter's bank account also in Dubai. A few years ago, one would see some business operations of US$4 million to US$5 million transiting through Djibouti to Somalia. Now this type of operation is less frequent in Djibouti than in Dubai.[6]

Even though Djibouti's role as a hub for financial operations related to Somalia has reportedly decreased, its geographic proximity to Somalia means it remains a base for financial operations in Somalia. That explains why a well-known MVTS operator in the region opened offices in Djibouti. The operator was looking for a place to open a bank for Somalia, but it wanted to do so in a country that had the infrastructure needed to liaise with both the outside world and Somalia.[7] Djibouti provided that venue. The bank also opened branches in Mogadishu, Bossaaso, and Hargeysa,[8] which are the three major economic cities of Somalia (South Central, Puntland, and Somaliland).

During a meeting on June 6, 2012, between the team and senior management of the aforementioned bank in Djibouti, the managers detailed their operational challenges and how they were coping with them. The prime concern was linked to Know Your Customer (KYC) and Customer Due Diligence (CDD) procedures, even though the bank mentioned cross-checking identities against the UN 1267 list[9] and the U.S. Office of Foreign Assets Control (OFAC) Specially Designated Nationals List (SDN List). Because of reported widespread circulation of fake identification documents, the bank said it was requiring its customers to have their identity vouched for by the community.[10] The Management of the bank said it perceived that riskier areas in this regard were Bossaaso and Mogadishu. For this reason, the bank has enhanced monitoring of its branches in these two areas.

According to the interviewees, the branch in Bossaaso has 300 accounts and employs local staff. It manages currency and savings accounts. Statistics on operations from this branch are sent to the headquarters in Djibouti on a daily basis. The management of the bank mentioned having no knowledge of its services being abused by criminals, and attributed this success to its tailored KYC and CDD procedures. It was also mentioned that the bank would be willing to cooperate with law enforcement authorities, should requests concerning pirate cases be shared. The interviewees further suggested that serial numbers of bills used to pay ransoms be collected and shared with financial institutions in the region, in order to help identify monies associated with pirate proceeds.

The team also met with management of a second bank, which also has operating links to Somalia.[11] The issue of conducting thorough KYC and CDD was also raised. The bank requests a permanent residence card, since its clients must be residents of Djibouti. Clients who claim to own a company are checked with the Djibouti Chamber of Commerce. However, the bank's main link with financial flows to and from Somalia comes from the fact that it also handles bank accounts of Somali transfer companies in Djibouti.

The role of Dubai-based financial institutions deserves close analysis, as well. However, the team was not able to conduct field visits to the United Arab Emirates (UAE) in that respect, despite repeated requests to do so.

Bank accounts can be used for direct transfer, or for shipping commodities. Reportedly, financiers used relatives' names or bank accounts to transfer and launder their proceeds. As was explained during a 2011 interview conducted with the East African Seafarers' Association Programme,

> For instance, a pirate makes US$100,000 and wants to invest it. He will call his cousin or a relative living abroad. This relative will open a bank account under his own name and the pirate will transfer the money on it. Then they will agree that the cousin will invest this money (which he sometimes thinks is legitimate money) or open a business, which he will run on behalf of the pirate. But the money can also be directly invested in a business already existing. The profit from this activity will be remitted to the pirate completely, or partly because the pirate will ask his cousin (or whoever is running his business abroad) to remit a certain amount to his mother or a relative needing financial support somewhere in Somalia.

How Are the Proceeds Moved?

Financial wire transfers have been reported in some ransom payments. For instance, in the cases of the MV Pompei and MV CEC Future (FATF 2011),[12] the negotiator reportedly accepted for himself a separate wire transfer deposited to a bank account he indicated to the negotiators working with the ship owner. Other bank accounts located outside of Somalia have been identified in the course of investigations on piracy.[13]

Since the financial routes to and from Somalia are linked to business routes, the mechanisms to move money unnoticed are also related to business vulnerabilities. The following section examines how some businesses are misused by pirate financiers.

Trade-Based Money Laundering

Businesses that ship goods can easily be used to transfer money. Over- or underinvoicing is an easy way, among others, to transfer money from one location to another.

For instance, financier X in location A wants to transfer his proceeds to location B. If he owns a business, X will request his counterpart Y to ship goods for an amount of US$100, for instance, while sending an invoice of US$120. X will use a legitimate source for the US$100 and include US$20 from an illegitimate source. See figure 6.1 for a visual representation of this scheme.

If, however, X does not own a business, he can ask intermediary Z in location A to use one of his usual transactions with country B. X will give the US$20 to Z, who will include them in the payment. See figure 6.2 for a visual representation

Figure 6.1 Overinvoicing Scheme without an Intermediary

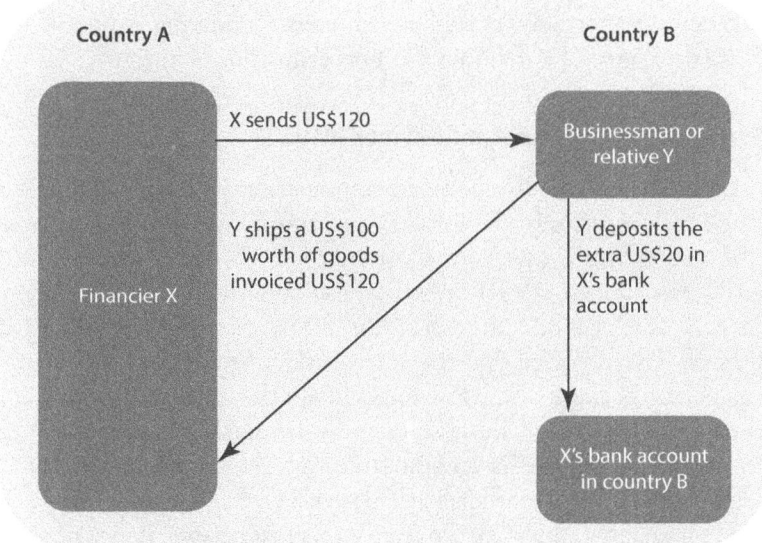

Source: Formulation based on discussions with the Seychelles Financial Intelligence Unit.
Note: The amounts used are for demonstration purposes only and do not represent actual proportions or amounts.

Figure 6.2 Overinvoicing Scheme with an Intermediary

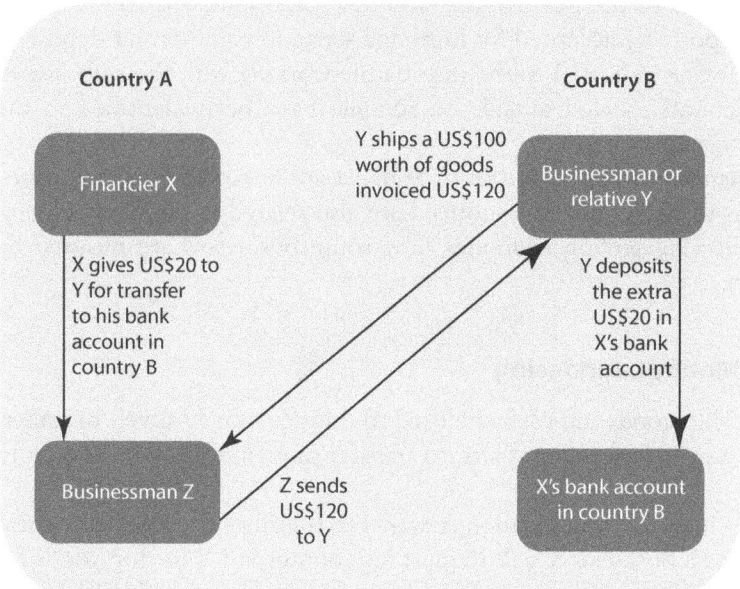

Source: Formulation based on discussions with the Seychelles Financial Intelligence Unit.
Note: The amounts used are for demonstration purposes only and do not represent actual proportions or amounts.

of this scheme. The end result is the same; the illegitimate US$20 will be transferred to location B, and, at the same time, will enjoy the status of legitimate funds since they now originate from a legitimate business transaction.

The only difference between using an intermediary or not, is that the use of an intermediary makes the whole transaction more difficult to trace by law enforcement agencies. Reportedly, trade-based money laundering is one of the main methods used to move and launder the proceeds from piracy.[14]

Misuse of Money or Value Transfer Services (MVTS)

Somali MVTS providers repeatedly claimed being unaware of funds from piracy transiting through their services.[15] They shared the same concerns as banks about the difficulty of conducting Know Your Customer (KYC) and Customer Due Diligence (CDD) procedures. MVTS providers also confirm their clients' identity against the UN 1267 list and the US OFAC SDN List for their offices in Western countries.[16] They insisted that they are conducting checks via the community in Somalia, also because of the low reliability of the identification system. However, reports on the abuse of these services by criminals, whether through money transfer or mobile transfer, have come from various sources (FATF 2011), ranging from reformed pirates, to officials in Puntland.[17]

One reformed pirate interviewed by the team explained his experience in moving money to acquire goods abroad.[18] He sent US$12,000 via a well-known MVTS provider in Puntland. The money was sent to Dubai to an intermediary who bought a car for him. The car was subsequently shipped to Somalia. He brought the US$12,000 to the MVTS office in US$50 and US$100 bills, which he said he got through *Shahaad*.[19] Other individuals present during that interview confirmed that one could buy a US$15,000 car in Dubai using MVTS in Puntland. However, in this case the operator was clearly abused, since the client had to justify the origin of his funds, and lied to the operator saying it came through charity.

Telecom financial services in Somalia are offered by various telecom companies operating in Somaliland, Puntland, and Southern and Central Somalia. During interviews with pirate inmates or reformed pirates, the team was informed that such services were used to move pirate proceeds inside Somalia. Even though most companies require an ID picture for each new customer,[20] and impose transaction limits of US$2,000 for individuals and US$100,000 for businesses, it is unclear how uniformly these limits are enforced. Field research in Somaliland has garnered allegations that no maximum threshold was actually enforced, and similar work in Puntland has garnered allegations that some companies could offer mobile transfer services ranging from US$80,000 to US$100,000. More information on the existence of a threshold and the (existing or potential) enforcement of such threshold is required. In Somaliland, it is estimated that 90 percent of the population uses online/telecom-based tools to handle their money transfer services (Shawky 2011).

A popular mobile telephone financial service in the region is the M-PESA service offered by the Kenyan-based company Safaricom. With respect to the cross-border movement of money, the team found that M-PESA does not engage in cross-border transfer of money to and from Somalia, and there have been no reports indicating that the Kenyan service is being misused by pirates.[21] Moreover, this service is monitored and regulated by the Central Bank of Kenya.

It is unclear how much MVTS providers know about the origin of the funds they transfer. As with other financial services, pirates probably abuse MVTS services without the provider's knowledge of the illegal origin of the funds, and, therefore, without their consent to facilitate illegal activities. There may be providers that are simply complicit, and that conduct the transactions even if they do know or suspect the illegal origins of the funds. It should be a priority to support MVTS providers that wish to operate within the law. In order to distinguish complicit companies from companies acting in good faith, genuine engagement with the private sector is needed.

Cross-Border Cash Smuggling

Moving money between Somalia and its neighboring countries can be done through cross-border transportation of cash. The porous nature of borders between Somalia and neighboring countries was a widely accepted fact by law enforcement agencies in the region. Several examples illustrate this. There is only one main customs checkpoint between Somaliland and Ethiopia, at Togochale.[22] The border between Ethiopia and Puntland was described by customs officials in the region[23] as "not adequately monitored," for the main reason that there is no concrete road. One official admitted that, because of the lack of adequate border controls, proceeds from piracy could potentially be used to destabilize Ethiopia, should the Ogaden National Revolutionary Front and pirates find a common interest in doing so. Incursion of Al-Shabaab fighters in the region of Wajir in 2010, the abductions of tourists on the Island of Lamu, and the kidnapping of Spanish aid workers in Dadaab in 2011, also pointed to the porosity of the borders between Kenya and Somalia.

In addition, the porous nature of borders is not limited to the Somali borders. For instance, while there are only three official border points between Lunga Lunga on the Kenya-Tanzania border and Mombasa, 812 unofficial routes in that region actually connect both destinations (Opala 2009a, 2009b). Ethiopia is struggling with similar issues. Smuggling through the borders of Djibouti was also reported to the team. According to officials,[24] each year, 70,000 illegal migrants cross through Djibouti from Ethiopia. Smugglers cross through the Republic of Yemen then to Saudi Arabia.

Another reported method of smuggling cash outside of Somalia is the use of aircraft,[25] which sometimes fly directly to foreign countries that accept large deposits of cash and that have few requirements or capacities in terms of cash disclosure at the border. There have been reported cases of cash payments made for khat transactions transported in this way.[26] This further confirms the fact that cash ransom monies are circulating outside of Somalia.

Thus, there appear to be numerous ways to move money outside and inside Somalia. Preferred methods inside Somalia for pirates and their financiers seem to be cash transportation or mobile banking. Trade-based money laundering or massive cash smuggling using aircraft are the two methods most reported to the team as used by financiers to move their proceeds outside of Somalia or to finance their operations.

Looking Forward: New Trends in Moving Money to and from Somalia

On October 27, 2009, one MVTS provider in the region launched its *eCash* service in Hargeisa.[27] The service offers credit and debit card payments to its customers. Transactions are made via the Internet for every bank account holder. The system is encrypted and protected by PIN (personal identification number) and signature control. Other financial service providers are planning to introduce credit and debit cards for Somalia. The service has yet to be implemented in the rest of Somalia. Other companies offer direct Internet wire transfer in over 30 countries (Shawky 2011). Both of these developments show that the financial sector in the region, and even inside Somalia, is more dynamic than one would think, and growing more quickly than state institutions are being developed. Law enforcement agencies and legislators need to be trained and updated on a regular basis in order to cope with potential misuses of these services.

The Central Banks in Somalia and "Somaliland"[28] have no capacity to monitor international transfers. The central banks in Somalia and "Somaliland" need urgent assistance and development, as well.

Law enforcement agencies in Somalia often do not have a good understanding of the exact mechanisms used in telecom-based financial transfers,[29] and need training on basic financial investigations. Simple issues, such as the analysis of SIM (Subscriber Identity Module) cards, depend on the goodwill of telecom companies to provide this service to law enforcement agencies.[30] Given the importance of telecom-based financial transfers in Somalia,[31] this is a concerning issue for the conduct and even the secrecy of investigations.

With such varied and effective capacities to move the money inside and out of Somalia, and limited monitoring capacities on the side of state authorities, financiers have a diverse range of options through which to launder their proceeds. The following chapters analyze the different reported uses and investments made with ransom proceeds.

Notes

1. Interview with pirates in custody, August 2012.
2. Interview with the Central Bank of Djibouti, June 4, 2012.
3. Interview with Senior Management of a commercial bank in Djibouti on June 4, 2012, and interviews in Hargeisa, November 2011.
4. Interview with the Central Bank of Djibouti, June 4, 2012.
5. Ibid.
6. Interview with Senior Management of a commercial bank in Djibouti on June 4, 2012.
7. Ibid.
8. http://www.dahabshilbank.com.
9. The list, was established and maintained pursuant to Security Council Resolutions 1267 (1999), 1333 (2000), 1390 (2002), as reiterated in resolutions 1455 (2003), 1526 (2004), 1617 (2005), 1735 (2006), 1822 (2008), 1904 (2009), and 1989 (2011) and contains the list of individuals, groups, undertakings, and other entities associated with Al-Qaida subject to asset freeze, travel ban, and other commercial sanctions.
10. Interview with bank officials in Djibouti.
11. Ibid.
12. In the case of the MV CEC Future, hijacked on November 7, 2008, a reported US$75,000 was wire transferred to the pirate negotiator in addition to US$1.7 million ransom paid in cash, which was airdropped in a predefined area on January 14, 2009. During the investigation related to the MV Pompei, hijacked on April 18, 2009, Belgian authorities identified bank accounts in the United Arab Emirates.
13. Address by representative of INTERPOL at a conference by the Cypriot Presidency of the European Union on Piracy, Larnaca, Cyprus, November 12–13, 2012.
14. Interview with the Financial Intelligence Unit of the Seychelles on Saturday August 9, 2012.
15. Minutes and Recommendations from the Second UNODC Conference on Illicit Financial Flows Linked to Piracy off the Coast of Somalia, held in Djibouti December 12–13, 2011, which focused on improving cooperation between MVTS and law

enforcement agencies. At the end of the conference, some of the MVTS providers confirmed that they would welcome assistance from the authorities to help them cope with potential misuse of their services, particularly providers of telecom-based financial services.

16. Minutes and Recommendations from the Second UNODC Conference on Illicit Financial Flows Linked to Piracy off the Coast of Somalia, held in Djibouti December 12–13, 2011, which focused on improving cooperation between MVTS and law enforcement agencies.
17. Correspondence received from Saeed Rage, Minister of Transport, Ports and Counter Piracy of the Puntland Federal State of Somalia, April 14, 2012.
18. Interview of the team with the Youth Organization Against Piracy, Garowe, Puntland, Sunday, April 8, 2012.
19. Traditional charity custom in Muslim societies, also spelled zekaat/zakat/زكاة.
20. http://golistelecom.com/our-services/sahal-service/. See also http://www.zaad.net/, http://e-maal.com/mmoney/soomali/Services/MobileMoneyTransfer/tabid/101/Default.aspx, http://hortel.net/home.php?readmore=52, and http://www.somtelnetwork.net/index.php?option=com_content&view=article&id=75&Itemid=61.
21. Interview with Safaricom, August 2012.
22. Interview with the Ethiopia Customs and Revenues Authority, also found at http://www.flickr.com/photos/danielzolli/4467852680/?q=togochale. *The immigration facilities are located 300 meters further into the village in an obscure room. So it isn't even possible to get your visa stamped directly at the border. However, most people (and animals) don't care, they just cross the border without any control. And many people do this, because of the famous market on the Somali side, where, for example, electronic goods are sold which aren't available in Ethiopia. Even people from Jijiga come here for that. The Ethiopian side is also attractive for the Somalis, because there are four banks in this village. The reason for that is that Somaliland—as an unrecognized state—doesn't have access to the international banking system, so some people manage their accounts through Ethiopian banks in Togochale.* Picture of the border: http://www.flickr.com/photos/danielzolli/4467082163/.
23. Interview of the team with customs officials in the region.
24. Interview with the Department of External Finance at the Djiboutian Ministry of Commerce.
25. UNODC communication with a western security source on June 15, 2012.
26. See chapter 8 on Khat.
27. http://www.dahabshiil.com/2009/10/dahabshiil-launches-new-electronic-cash-system.html.
28. Somaliland is a northern region considered a territory of the Federal State of Somalia in the Somali Constitution. However, the territory has been claiming its independence since 1991. Even though it has not been recognized as a sovereign independent state by the international community so far, Somaliland has been governed as an autonomous territory by its own administration since it claimed independence.
29. Interview with Somaliland Officials in Hargeysa, October 2011.
30. Interview with Somaliland Officials in Hargeysa, October 2011.
31. According to the World Bank's Global Findex Database, over 30 percent of the Somali population uses mobile money transfers (Demirguc-Kunti and Klapper 2012, 1–58).

CHAPTER 7

How Do Pirate Financiers Invest Their Proceeds?

Overview of Reported Pirate Financiers' Investments within Somalia

The vast majority of the pirate financiers identified by the team are located inside Somalia. Their profiles vary and include former police and military officers, khat dealers, former fishermen, former businessmen or civil servants, and successful pirates-turned financiers. Some financiers are also located abroad, as explained below.

The following analysis is based on data collected for this report, but it is anticipated that reporting, as it stands, is incomplete to the extent that there is no way of knowing whether the sample is representative of the totality of investments or not. More research needs to be conducted by law enforcement and intelligence agencies, to gather a more precise accounting of these assets, especially assets located outside of Somalia. Using available data, this section presents a preliminary outline of the main features that can be deduced about Somali pirate financiers. Keeping in mind the different networks and their evolution in time, as presented earlier in this study,[1] the following analysis also presents the evolution of these investments in order to try to understand the impact and potential developments of pirate networks in Somalia.

Two analyses were developed based on the dataset on pirate financiers presented in the methodological framework section of this report. The first focuses on the sample of 59 financiers[2] spreading across Somalia. The second analysis allows for a more dynamic approach, comparing investments made by pirate financiers active south of Galkayo and investments made by pirate financiers active north of Galkayo.

The map presented in map 7.1 shows the main reported locations of pirate financiers' assets in Eastern Africa and, principally, inside Somalia. The intensity of colors used for each location reflects the number of assets reported—a darker-colored circle corresponds to a higher number of assets that were reported to the team as belonging to or working for pirate financiers.[3]

Map 7.1 Reported Locations of Pirate Financiers' Assets in Eastern Africa

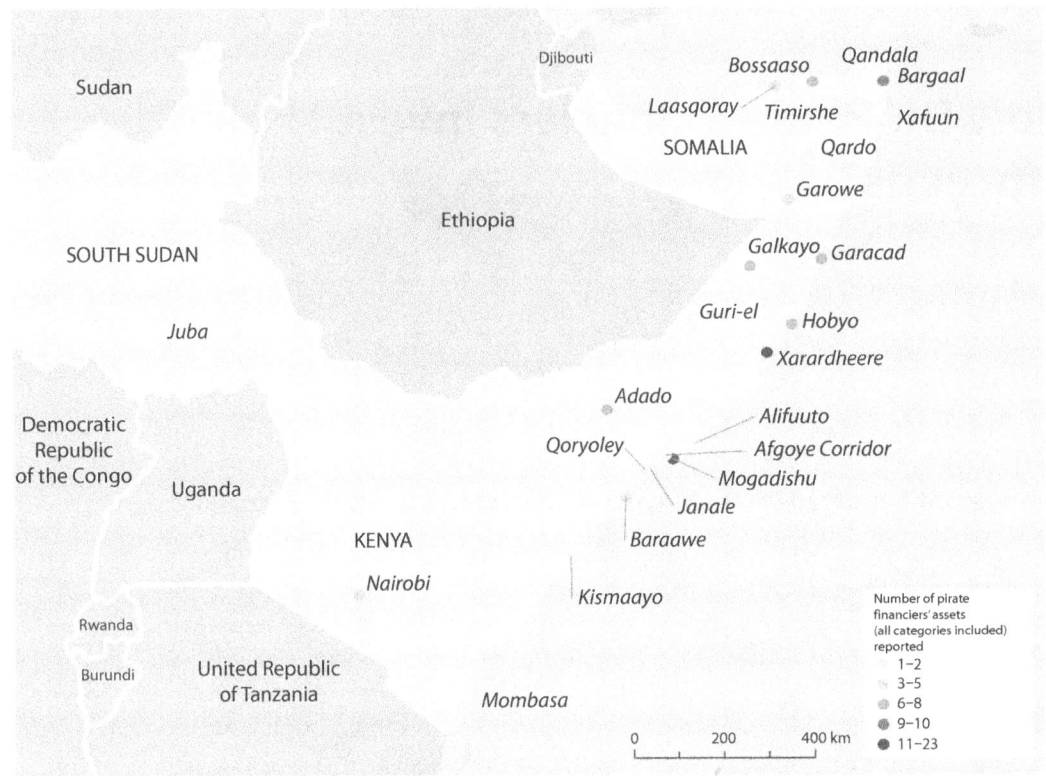

Source: UNODC 2012. © United Nations. Used with permission; further permission required for re-use.
Note: The boundaries and names shown and the designations used on this map do not imply official endorsement or acceptance by the United Nations. Dashed lines represent undetermined boundaries. The final boundary between the Republic of Sudan and the Republic of South Sudan has not yet been determined.

Data show that, contrary to conventional wisdom, many investments are actually made within Somalia. This does not mean, however, that the majority of the money is laundered or reinvested inside Somalia. In this precise case, it should be clear that the discrepancy between the number of assets identified inside Somalia and the number of assets identified outside is due to a lack of reporting to the team by concerned states, or by stakeholders with knowledge of such assets outside of Somalia. Therefore, the data reproduced are only the data available. Several factors can explain the unwillingness of some actors to share information, primarily the confidentiality of ongoing investigations.

What the following map shows, however, is that criminal proceeds invested in Somalia are not limited to a single region. Furthermore, some actors possess a substantial number of assets inside Somalia, reinforcing concerns over a criminal influence on the economy especially at a time when peace and security start returning to Somalia, further allowing economic growth to develop.[4]

An unexpected result is that the area where pirates most commonly invest money seems to be the development of militias or political influence.[5] After this

How Do Pirate Financiers Invest Their Proceeds?

item come "traditional" sectors for money laundering, such as hotels, restaurants, and real estate. It is also striking to see that, beyond investing in their own operations, some pirate financiers also provide other financial services, as accountants, as advisors, or by the provision of loans. Thirteen pirate financiers are reportedly providing such services, showing quite a degree of education and sophistication in the way they conduct their business and manage their proceeds (UNODC 2012). At a time when the political process in Mogadishu is showing encouraging signs of progress,[6] the potential development of a well-organized and heavily armed criminal network, fueled by the proceeds from piracy, and potentially mingling[7] with insurgent groups active in the region (Garowe Online 2012a; Mubarak 2011), cannot be overlooked.

Investments in Legitimate Business Activities

Proceeds from piracy can be laundered through direct investments in legitimate businesses, including real estate. Such investments concern businesses as far away as Europe and Eastern Africa and Asia,[8] ranging from small retail stores, restaurants, and gas stations (UNODC 2012) to joint ventures or even factories.[9] Piracy is no exception.

As shown in figure 7.1, the third most commonly reported area of investment by pirate financiers is the transport business. Specifically, the primary type of "transports" rented by financiers in the studied sample is supplying boats for pirate attacks (UNODC 2012). The dataset also shows that some pirates choose to invest in truck companies. These investments in transport and logistics can easily be explained by a need to supply logistics for pirate operations.

Figure 7.1 Number of Investors Engaging in Activity

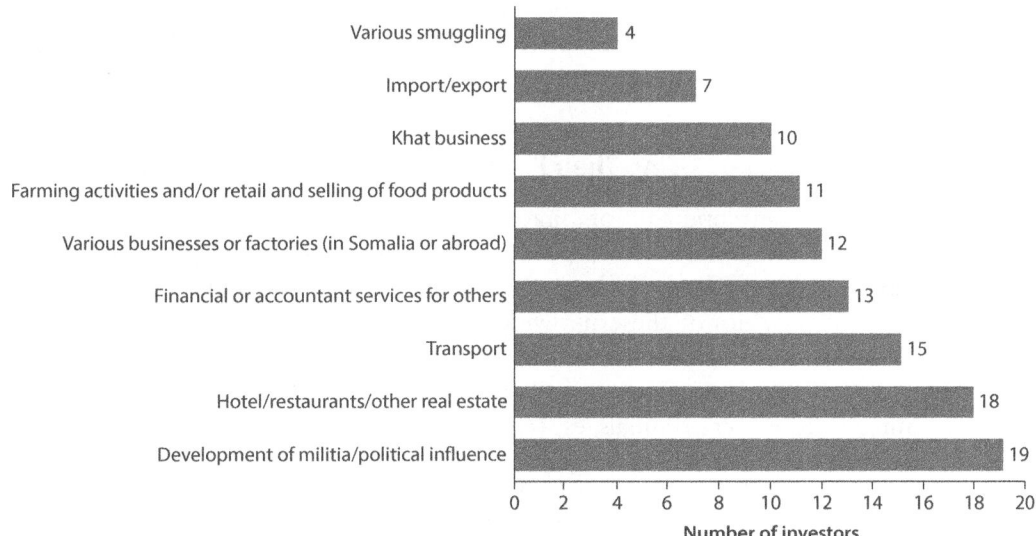

Source: UNODC 2012.

Among the 15 financiers investing in various transport services, at least four of them invested their proceeds in the oil business, supplying fuel to pirates (UNODC 2012). There seems to be a wider interest of the Somali community in the oil business within East Africa. In Kenya, the petroleum market is a free entry and exit market, mostly controlled by the Kenyan Energy Board.[10] According to experts from the Kenyan Revenue Authority, interviewed by the team in Nairobi, Somalis began entering this market in 2007, at the wholesale, distribution, and transportation levels. However, no information has been gathered or reported thus far that would indicate links between the oil supplied by pirate financiers inside Somalia and members of the diaspora running such businesses.

Some pirates have started to offer their services as consultants or experts on piracy (United Nations 2012a), negotiators for victims or shipping companies, and providers of other services, including proof-of-life interviews. Material obtained by the UNODC during this study demonstrates that these "companies" openly advertise their services, sending invoices, advertising their services or even contacting victims of hijackings directly. Their members are former pirates, members of the diaspora, and facilitators, or even have ties with militias (United Nations 2012a).

Other companies with suspected ties to former pirates[11] focus on security aboard vessels. Somali maritime security companies have long existed independently from piracy (Bahadur 2011). They seem to provide their services to smaller embarkation such as small cargo or fishing dhows owned by companies that do not have the means to hire a professional private security company, or even to contract an insurer. As one informed individual put it, "We have seen at least one Yemeni fishing vessel with three Somali crew members. When we asked the other crew members who they were, one of them advised us that they were private security."[12]

However, the formal ties between these companies and pirate financiers, and whether proceeds from piracy were used to set up such companies, need further substantiation and research.

Pirate Financiers Using Their Proceeds for Other Criminal Activities

The latest developments of pirate operations indicate a growing activity of financiers and pirate leaders operating north of Galkayo (UNODC-WB 2012). This evolution raises concerns about the different investment patterns and criminal activities of these networks. Reports showing an increased link with insurgent groups pushed from the south of Somalia to the north were shared with the team.[13] Also, networks located north of Galkayo tend to more easily mingle with other criminals, especially pirate networks operating in the area of Bargaal (UNODC 2012). In addition, as developed in the coming section, these networks are also investing more heavily in militias and military capacities on land.

Networks Investing in Land-Based Militias: Dynamic Analysis of Investments by Financiers Operating South of Galkayo Compared to Investments by Financiers Operating North of Galkayo

As shown in figure 7.2, financiers operating north of Galkayo are more inclined to invest in militias and political influence than financiers operating south of Galkayo; 7 financiers have reportedly made such investment in the South compared to 12 in the North. This development can be explained by two factors. The first is that these networks experienced confrontation from local communities, as evidenced in the port city of Eyl, whose residents chased pirates out of the city.[14] Therefore, pirate financiers with their own militia have more influence over communities that might attempt to reject them. A second explanation of increased military activities on land is the involvement of pirate operators in kidnapping for ransom on land. At the time of drafting this report, the most recent kidnapping on land within Somalia had taken place in Bacadweyne, 45 kilometers north of Galkayo, on July 11, 2011, when three Kenyan aid workers of the International Aid Service were kidnapped.

However, kidnappings on land are not limited to pirate networks operating north of Galkayo. In the Report of the Monitoring Group on Somalia and Eritrea pursuant to Security Council Resolution 2002 (2011), the Monitoring Group identifies several members of the Hobyo-Xarardheere networks allegedly involved in kidnapping in the Somali hinterland: Ahmed Garfanje, Afweyne, Ahmed Sanaag, Hussein Jiis, Suhuffi and Abdiqadir Mohamed Abdi. Concerns over the expansion of pirate activities on land were already expressed at the political level when the Contact Group on Piracy off the Coast of Somalia, in its

Figure 7.2 Number of Pirate Financiers Engaging in Activity North and South of Galkayo

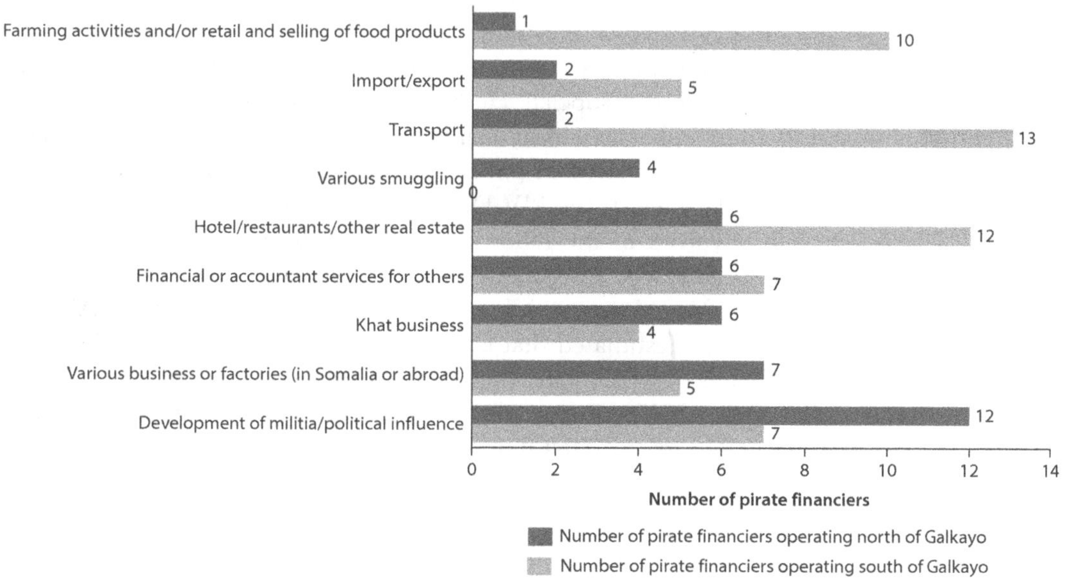

Activity	North of Galkayo	South of Galkayo
Farming activities and/or retail and selling of food products	1	10
Import/export	2	5
Transport	2	13
Various smuggling	4	0
Hotel/restaurants/other real estate	6	12
Financial or accountant services for others	6	7
Khat business	6	4
Various business or factories (in Somalia or abroad)	7	5
Development of militia/political influence	12	7

Source: UNODC 2012.

communiqué released at its twelfth plenary meeting in New York, raised "concern over the potential expansion of criminal activities on land, in particular the kidnapping of humanitarian workers and civilians, by networks involved in piracy."[15]

While the international community is trying to build on the momentum boosting the political process in Mogadishu following the adoption of the Federal Constitution and the successful election of President Hassan Sheikh Mohamud, attention should be paid to these developing criminal networks on land. If these networks, fueled by proceeds from piracy, are not targeted and their financial capacities disrupted, they may well represent a threat to international staff entering and working in Somalia. Furthermore, the networks investing the most in militias are reportedly located in Puntland, where individual cases of operational cooperation between pirate financiers and Al-Shabaab were reported to the team.[16] The subsequent risk is the increasing destabilization of Puntland by these networks (Garowe Online 2012b; Mubarak 2011), thereby jeopardizing all the improvements gained in the South since the beginning of 2012.

Case Study: Ciise Yulux, Piracy, Khat, and Interclan Conflicts in Puntland

As early as 2009, the United Nations Monitoring Group on Somalia confirmed that "Ransoms from piracy and kidnapping [had] been used to finance arms embargo violations" (Garowe Online 2012a; Mubarak 2011). During an interview with Government of Puntland officials in Garowe, concern was expressed about relations between pirates and the insurgent group Al-Shabaab.[17] As mentioned above, of the sample of 59 financiers studied for this report, 19 were said to use their proceeds to develop militias or political influence, with 12 reportedly operating in Puntland (North of Galkayo).

The case of Ciise Yulux[18] illustrates how proceeds from piracy can represent a threat to the stability and security of Somalia. Ciise Yulux is a member of the Majerteen/Cali Saleebaan subclan. He has been a pirate since at least 2007. He is originally from Rakoraaxa, near Gardo in the Bari region.[19] Ciise Yulux is known to have been involved in piracy attacks against the MV Buccaneer, the MV Leila, the MV Eleni P, the MV Dover, and the SY ING Kalundborg,[20] and was allegedly involved in the following cases:[21] MV Amiya Scan, MV Stella Maris, MV Blue Star, MV Al-Nisr Al Saud, MV Buccaneer, MV Thor Star, MV Golden Blessing, MV Motivator, CEC MV Future, MV Theresa Viii, MV Talca, and EMS River. It is estimated that altogether these cases generated US$49.62 million in ransoms of which Ciise Yulux would have collected at least US$5.65 million (UNODC 2012). Reportedly, Ciise Yulux is also engaged in the khat business in the Bari region (UNODC 2012).

Following the Buccaneer case, a fight between Ciise Yulux and one of his main partners, Omar Hassan Osman (also known as Baqalayo), ensued. Baqalayo is allegedly the son of a pirate called Hanano from Warsengeli/Reer Haaji, who used to operate in Laasqoray in 2009 (UN 2010). While dividing the ransom proceeds received from the attack against the MV Bucaneer, the pirates began fighting and one of Yulux's followers was killed (Micalessin Gian 2009). Following the fight, Baqalayo's subclan refused to pay the blood debt to the Cali Saleebaan subclan.[22]

This started an interclan fight, which reportedly prompted Baqalayo to import weapons to Somalia, and Baqalayo and Yulux also reportedly attempted to kill each other on several occasions.[23] In November 2009, Puntland Police Forces arrested Baqalayo. He is currently serving a 15-year sentence in the prison of Bossaaso (UN 2010).

Clan fighting related to the Cali Saleebaan subclan in the region of Gardo continued to spread to other subclans, to include the Ali Jibrahil subclan. On July 27, 2011, the main leaders of the Cali Saleebaan subclan met in Dubai, the United Arab Emirates, and officially withdrew their support from the Puntland Government (Dharoor.com 2011). On July 30, 2011, the Puntland Government stated it was "fed up" with clan fighting and deployed 1,200 soldiers around Ufeyn (Abdi 2011). However, despite this first intervention, the Puntland President had to engage in another mediation effort in March 2012, with clan leaders in Gardo—capital of the Bari region, where Ufeyn and Rakoraaxa are located (Garowe Online 2012d)—in order to resolve the ongoing crisis.

Deteriorating security and government instability related to interclan fighting are not the only by-products of piracy and the proceeds gained through piracy ransom payments. Ciise Yulux reportedly commands a force of around 50 militiamen (UNODC 2012), possesses several *Technicals* (pick-up cars equipped with mounted automatic weapons), and is now operating from Caalula and Hul Anod (UNODC 2012). This is a conservative assessment, since open sources estimate that "Yulux runs a militia of around 70 men on land and sea. Another 50 reserves are based in Timishre. They operate about seven Toyota technical, 50 AKs, 20 PKM's, 11 RPGs and around seven Dshka's" (Pelton 2012). According to credible sources,[24] in the first quarter of 2012, Yulux was providing money and equipment to fighters linked to Al-Qaeda in the Arabian Peninsula and Al-Shabaab, transiting to the Republic of Yemen.[25]

Yulux's cooperation with Al-Shabaab must be differentiated from other known pirate financial arrangements between pirates and the militant group. Pirates based in the Hobyo-Xarardheere network,[26] and other pirates operating in Al-Shabaab-controlled areas, are paying a "development tax" (various names are given in the existing literature) (Mubarak 2011; UN 2011a; and interview of the team with Minister Rage in Garowe, Puntland, April 2012) to Al-Shabaab in order to access the port. Protection money is also paid and occasional cooperation can occur in the form of access to equipment and/or weaponry (UNODC 2011a). However, no strategic cooperation has been observed for these networks.[27] In the case of Ciise Yulux, however, reporting indicates a direct involvement of Yulux during Al-Shabaab operations, facilitating movements of alleged jihad fighters.[28] There is, in this respect, a clear threat of operational cooperation[29] between some senior Al-Shabaab figures and financiers of piracy, when the same person does not already conduct both activities.[30]

While this last concern was made pretty clear to the team by some senior officials in Eastern Africa and the Horn of Africa, they could not be further substantiated.

The case of Ciise Yulux shows the multiple influences that pirate monies have over the stability and political environment of Somalia, beyond ongoing allegations of corruption. In this case, a single pirate leader is using his criminal proceeds to (a) invest in the khat business, (b) build up his own capacities as a warlord, (c) fuel clan rivalries in Somalia, and (d) provide operational support to Al-Shabaab.

Pirate Financiers Engaging in Smuggling and Trafficking

As shown in figure 7.1, at least four pirate financiers are reportedly engaging in various smuggling activities. Of these, at least two are engaging in human trafficking and/or migrant smuggling. One case was reported where the same PAG hijacked a vessel after having dropped people on the Yemeni coast and while on its way back to Somalia.[31] Analyzing operational links between pirates and migrant smugglers may require further research, since the information is scarce beyond reports of skiffs simultaneously carrying out several crimes. For instance, the team also interviewed a convicted pirate, in Kenya, who acknowledged that, before engaging in piracy, he had served as liaison between Puntland and the Republic of Yemen, smuggling migrants on his way to the Republic of Yemen and bringing weapons to Somalia on his return. According to Chris Horwood, coordinator of the Regional Mixed Migrations Secretariat,[32] which monitors flows of migrants between the Republic of Yemen and the Horn of Africa, proceeds generated annually by smugglers operating from Bossaaso to the Republic of Yemen amount to approximately US$3 million per year,[33] which is what pirates received on average for each successfully hijacked vessel and released for ransom between 2005 and 2012 (UNODC-WB 2012).[34]

The risks for smugglers at the foot-soldier level are lower than for pirates, since the risk of death is lower and the duration of an operation drops from weeks or months to 8 to 15 hours.[35] In addition, each skiff from Bossaaso to the Republic of Yemen makes approximately US$9,000, and there are fewer actors sharing the proceeds (no militia ashore, no catering services, and so forth).[36] Foot soldiers of piracy (especially if they own their skiffs) could therefore find some interest in turning to migrant smuggling. Indeed, while a pirate foot soldier will potentially make between US$30,000 and US$75,000, at best, after a successful mission, (which can take up to several months, or a year by the time the ransom is paid), a smuggler foot soldier can hope to share proceeds of US$9,000 among a smaller number of people (himself and his sponsor) in a single journey to the Republic of Yemen.

As explained in the first section of chapter 5 of this report, pirates spend their proceeds not only on khat, cars, and alcohol but also on trafficked girls and sex workers or even sex slaves. In several interviews, the team was informed that girls as young as 14 were being trafficked for "pirate consumption." While it was also reported that some women would engage of their own free will with pirates, several cases were reported to the team of young girls being trafficked to forcibly work as sex slaves (see detailed case studies in appendix A).

Pirate financiers spend their proceeds on a wide range of activities, both legitimate and criminal, including on trafficked and smuggled human beings and on buying weapons, alcohol, khat, alcohol, real estate, and companies. It is striking, however, how sophisticated and cunning some of these investments may be. Engaging in counterpiracy is probably the boldest of all, but most concerning is the fact that pirate financiers have now evolved to the point where they are not only the most successful criminals at sea but also some of the most powerful actors on land, thanks to their weaponry and economic influence.

The following chapter provides an in-depth analysis of two sectors to which the proceeds of piracy are reportedly flowing, and which have ties to other countries in the region: khat and real estate.

Notes

1. See chapter 3, section on "Somali Pirate Networks."
2. See chapter 2, Methodological Framework, UNODC dataset on pirate financiers.
3. See chapter 2, Methodological Framework, UNODC dataset on pirate financiers. By asset is meant the number of buildings, real estate, or other businesses in a given location.
4. See chapter 3 section on "Criminal Influence on the Economy."
5. This breakdown of pirate financiers' expenditures does not conflict with the breakdown presented in the World Bank Report (2013); the present analysis focuses solely on the investments made by pirate financiers (representing 30–50 percent of the total amount paid in ransom), while the World Bank Report analysis focuses on the total amount paid in ransom, therefore aggregating the figures that are broken down in the present analysis.
6. See chapter 3 section on Current Situation in Somalia.
7. Interviews of the team with Puntland Officials in Garowe, Puntland, April 8–9, 2012.
8. Interview with the Financial Intelligence Unit of the Seychelles on Saturday August 9, 2012.
9. Interviews of the team with Puntland Officials in Garowe, Puntland, April 8–9, 2012.
10. Interview with the Kenyan Revenue Authority, May 31, 2012.
11. Interview of the team with Rear-Admiral Jean-Baptise Dupuis, then Commander of the European Union Naval Force, Djibouti, June 3, 2012.
12. Interview of the team with Rear-Admiral Jean-Baptise Dupuis, then Commander of the European Union Naval Force, Djibouti, June 3, 2012.
13. Interviews of the team with Puntland Officials in Garowe, Puntland, April 8–9, 2012.
14. UNODC interviews in Bossaaso, October 2011.
15. Communiqué (accessed November 18, 2012), http://www.thecgpcs.org/plenary.do?action=plenarySub&seq=21.
16. Interviews of the team with Puntland officials in Garowe, Puntland, April 8–9, 2012.

17. Interviews in April 2012.
18. Also known as Isse Mohamoud Yusuf, Isse Yuluh, Isse Yulux, Esse Yuluh, Esse Yulux, and Issa Yuhluw.
19. UNODC interviews in Puntland.
20. UNODC correspondence with a Western security source, July 2012.
21. UNODC communication with a Western security source.
22. UNODC interviews in Puntland.
23. Ibid.
24. Interviews of the team with Puntland officials in Garowe, Puntland, April 8–9, 2012.
25. Even though Ciise Yulux is mingling with Al-Shabaab, the whole Cali Saleeban sub-clan should not be associated with Al-Shabaab. A declaration of Cali Saleeban elders in the United Arab Emirates, whereby they officially withdrew their support to the Puntland Government, did not mention anything that would point toward religious conservatism; it actually accuses the Puntland Government of having failed to promote gender equality, for instance. Also, despite the tensions between the Cali Saleebaan subclan and the Government of Puntland, Minister of Finance Dr. Farah Ali Jama, who is a member of the Cali Saleebaan, has never had to leave his functions as minister. In addition, several officials (including the Minister of Fisheries, the Minister of Peace-Keeping, and the Leader of the Bari region) attended a meeting of the Cali Saleebaan in Bossaaso, in late June 2012. This meeting was held at the Panorama Hotel in Bossaaso with about 200 participants who came for the introduction of a newly elected Sultan in the Cali Saleeban, Sultan Maxamuud Xasan Cumar, who assumed his functions on behalf of the seven-year-old son of the deceased Sultan Ciise Xasan Cumar. See http://horseedmedia.net/2012/06/15/suldaanka-beesha-biciidyah-an-cali-saleebaan-oo-boosaaso-lagu-caleema-saaray-sawiro/ (accessed July 24, 2012, and November 7, 2012).
26. As defined by the June 2011 Report of the Monitoring Group on Somalia and Eritrea pursuant to Security Council Resolution 1916 (2010) to the United Nations Security Council
27. In that sense, the team shares the assessment made by the UNSEMG in their June 2011 report.
28. Interviews of the team with Puntland officials in Garowe, Puntland, April 8–9, 2012
29. See also Do et al. (2013).
30. Interviews of the team with Puntland officials in Garowe, Puntland, April 8–9, 2012, confirmed by other confidential sources.
31. Communication with a Regional Anti-Piracy Prosecution Intelligence Coordination Centre (RAPPICC) analyst on March 11, 2013. (The group seemed to have taken migrants across the Gulf of Aden in a whaler-type vessel that was towing a second empty skiff. They dropped the migrants off near the Yemeni coast then returned to the Puntland coast. They encountered the PRAMONI in the International Recommended Transit Corridor and made an opportunistic and successful attack. The PRAMONI was hijacked on January 1, 2010, in position 12 31N 047 17E and was released on February 26, 2010. For the majority of its period of captivity it was held at Eyl.)
32. The Regional Mixed Migration Secretariat is funded by the European Commission with additional support from the Swiss Development Cooperation, the International Organisation for Migration, and the British government.

33. The business taking irregular migrants to the Republic of Yemen was worth at least US$16 million in 2011 and 2012—US$3 million from Bossaaso and US$13 million from Djibouti (UNODC Communication with Chris Horwood, January 16, 2013).
34. The exact average is US$ 3.06 million.
35. Communication with Chris Horwood, January 16, 2013.
36. Communication with Chris Horwood, January 16, 2013.

CHAPTER 8

Khat and Real Estate

The khat network reaches every corner of Somalia every day of the year and doesn't stop for wars, drought, floods, epidemics, Friday prayers, Ramadan—anything really.[1]

Khat[2]

Khat is a small, leafy plant that when chewed induces a mild state of euphoria and stimulation. Among communities in the Horn of Africa, the Arabian Peninsula, and in particular in Somalia, the chewing of khat is part of a social custom dating back thousands of years. The trade in khat is worth hundreds of millions of dollars a year (Dirie 2012). While khat is a controlled substance or considered an illegal substance in some countries such as the United States, the trade in khat remains legal in other countries including Ethiopia, Kenya, Somalia, the United Kingdom, and the Republic of Yemen. The khat trade is well monitored in Djibouti and Ethiopia but is not monitored in Kenya, and is more susceptible to inflows from proceeds of piracy. Hence, the team decided to focus on the khat trade in Kenya. (See appendix B for a description of the khat business.)

Khat Trade in Kenya

Traditionally, Kenya has been the major supplier of khat to neighboring Somalia, with virtually all Kenyan khat originating from the district area of Maua in Meru County, Mount Kenya Region,[3] where local farmers have been harvesting the plant for centuries.[4] One of the farmers with whom the team spoke suggested that khat growing in the region dated as far back as 1882. Because the active ingredient in harvested khat breaks down very quickly (about 48 hours after picking), the trade in khat is dependent on a highly efficient and rapid distribution network. This network has developed over the decades and involves many players, including the farmers who grow the khat, the middlemen who buy the khat in markets in Kenya, drivers who are responsible for ensuring its swift delivery, and local carrier companies who fly it into Somalia and other foreign airports.

The Somali community has maintained strong control over this trade, particularly the distribution network.[5] Despite the logistical challenges of khat delivery, it has remained a significant trade and is a sizable portion of Somalia's imports (Kimenyi 2010[6]; Maimbo 2006, 6; Omar 2012). The concern is that pirates are buying into the khat trade and using it as a way to launder the proceeds of piracy underpinned by control that Somalis have over the distribution network of the khat trade.

Piracy and Khat

There is lack of official data, since khat growing is an unregulated sector in Kenya. The analysis below is based on a visit made by the team to Maua, and on interviews held with people who are involved with and have knowledge of the khat trade.

In an interview the team had with airport officials at the Wilson Airport just outside Nairobi, it is estimated that around 3,000 kilos of khat are flown out of Kenya three times a day to Mogadishu (that is 3,000 × 3 = 9,000 kilograms),[7] throughout the year. Therefore, about 3.285 million kilograms[8] of khat are exported annually to Mogadishu alone. Moreover, the team was informed by some farmers in Maua and in interviews with public and private sector players with knowledge of the khat business that while there are other sources of khat that is exported to Puntland, the bulk of it is imported from Kenya.

Pirate communities, in particular, are known to use khat and are willing to pay higher prices for it. While khat is sold for about US$50 per kilo in the streets of coastal cities, pirates can pay up to three times the normal market price, reaching US$150 per kilo (UN 2011a, confirmed during the team's interviews with pirate inmates in Mombasa and the Seychelles). Consequently, an important part of the money earned by pirate foot soldiers goes to buying khat.

Since the khat trade is a very lucrative business (Kimenyi 2010; Omar 2012), it is not surprising that numerous reports indicate that the khat trade is partially funded by ransom money from pirates. While pirates buy the khat for consumption purposes (see chapter 5), several pirate financiers are also investing in it. As shown in chapter 7 (figure 7.1), at least 10 pirate financiers are engaging in this activity.

Given the predominant cash-based nature of transactions in the khat business, it is easy for pirates to buy into the business and for ransom money to be laundered through the khat trade. It is reported that one of the fathers of piracy, Mohamed Abdi Hassan (also known as Afweyne) has publicly retired from piracy, and is now engaged and invests heavily in khat trade (UN 2011a). The pirate warlord Cisse Yulux is also reportedly engaged in the khat business in the Bari region (UNODC 2012).

During interviews with convicted pirates, the team was told that the importance of pirate money in the khat trade is such that it has changed the organization of that trade. According to them, it used to be a cooperative type of business, whereby several investors would organize shipments of khat to a certain region.

With the involvement of pirates, who have enough cash to operate their own distribution networks, former pirates have taken over former khat cooperatives. Furthermore, pirate financiers have access to pirate markets, where the khat is sold at higher prices, thereby enhancing their profits.

Since consolidators in Somalia fix the prices of khat when they communicate their demand to brokers in Kenya, the increased role of pirate financiers or former pirate financiers in the khat trade also means that these actors have an increasing influence over the economy of Maua, in Kenya where the khat is produced.

The Real Estate Market

Laden with sacks of cash, these rogue investors were said to be converting illegally acquired ransom bounty into commercial and residential real estate.[9]

During a taxi ride from the airport to a downtown hotel in one of the countries in the Horn of Africa, one of the members of the team conversed with the taxi driver about the political, social, and economic issues relevant to the country. The taxi driver lamented the skyrocketing prices of houses in the country. Asked what the main reason was for this, he retorted, "Oh, it is money coming from the piracy activities in Somalia." Moreover, he continued, he was aware of situations where the price of houses tripled or quadrupled over the last few years. This is a refrain and complaint heard from a majority of people across all levels of society in the region and even in the international media.

However, is this the reality? Or is there more to the real estate boom than what is claimed in the streets and office corridors? When available data from both the formal and informal economy (see details in appendix C) are reviewed, the increase in the price of houses appears more likely to be due to a number of factors unrelated to piracy. Analysis of the available data shows that bank credit and remittances from the diaspora are major sources of finance in the purchase of real estate in Kenya and elsewhere in the region.

It is the study's finding that the US$413 million pirates made between 2005 and 2012 is a drop in the ocean compared to the bank credit and remittance flows into the real estate sector. In Kenya, for example, the annual bank credit to the real estate sector was US$491 million, and for Ethiopia, an estimated US$2.3 billion is remitted annually by the diaspora, with a significant portion being invested in the real estate sector. Consequently, the ransom payments cannot influence the property prices, as is suggested by many in the public and private sectors.

Piracy Financial Flows and Real Estate

Any discussion of financial flows from piracy activities should take into count that there are many drivers of the exponential growth in the real estate market. Even while the property market in most of the developed world collapsed in the wake of the 2008 financial crisis, the property market in the emerging and developing economies has seen an overall boom (Kaufman 2012). For most developing economies, investing in the real estate market is a primary way to safeguard one's savings from inflationary pressures and a reliable investment with a good return (Geetha and Ramesh 2011). The Horn of Africa and Eastern African regions are not an exception to this real estate sector boom (Kabukuru 2012).

This study finds that the available data suggest that this perception of proceeds of piracy fueling the real estate growth especially in Kenya is an exaggeration. The available and accessible data for the real estate market in the region indicate that the main drivers of the property boom are credit by the banking sector to the real estate market, flows of remittances from the diaspora, and general supply and demand of housing units. There is no information to support the perception that proceeds from piracy has been a factor. Such a perception is driven primarily by the media and general public sentiment. (See appendix C for a detailed discussion of these drivers.)

However, we do not know what percentage of real estate is financed through bank credit and remittances or what exactly are the other sources of financing in the real estate sector. In order to understand this, there need to be more data available in terms of the total volume of transactions for the real estate sector. This is where a challenge arises, because in most developing countries, certainly in Sub-Saharan Africa, data on the total volume of real estate transactions in a given period are not compiled. Walley writing on housing finance in "Financial Sector Development in Africa" says, "there is a vast black hole in available data relating to housing needs, housing construction levels, and housing quality in Africa" (Beck and Maimbo 2013, 118). Consequently, this lack of data makes it difficult to calculate a percentage for the bank credit/remittances share of financing in the real estate sector.

This missing link calls for further research, as mentioned below, in understanding the nature of financing in the real estate sector. Were this possible, it would provide a clear sense of what are the known legitimate financial sources and what might be the percentage of illegitimate financial sources of the real estate sector in the region.

Suspicion of Ransom Payments in the Real Estate Sector

Upon consideration of the above-mentioned factors that have influenced real estate prices, it is important to consider the accuracy of the perception that proceeds generated from piracy are also a significant contributing factor. As a result of the opacity of money transfers into and out of Somalia, it is inherently more difficult to determine the flow of cash into the real estate sector and its source (Manson 2012). Indeed, a January 2013 report (Ayieko 2013) in the *Daily Nation*, one of Kenya's top newspapers, cited concerns expressed by the head of the Central Bank of Kenya about the source of the money behind the boom in the country's real estate sector. The governor of the Central Bank was quoted as saying that "there is something wrong somewhere that needs to be investigated. Where is the money coming from?" (Ayieko 2013).

It is possible that a portion of ransom money from piracy is laundered through various sectors in the economies of the region. Laundering channels can be through legitimate businesses such as the hotel industry, the food industry, the khat business and, indeed, the real estate sector. Considering that an estimated US$340 million to US$413 million has been generated from piracy activities over the last seven years, it is not inconceivable that some of the proceeds would have been channeled through the real estate sector in the region. Nevertheless, the information to support such a perception is not available and is driven primarily by confidential reports, the media, and general public sentiment. As shown in figure 7.1, at least 18 pirate financiers have reportedly made such investments (UNODC 2012), which is enough to conclude that some money goes to the real estate sector, but is definitely not sufficient to say precisely where, and even less to point to any investment of such importance that it would influence the market's prices. In addition, some reports suggest that the proceeds from ransoms are spent or invested outside Kenya (Walley 2011, 18).

It will be important to look into how individuals in the region or a particular jurisdiction in the region finance the purchase of real estate. It will be critical to be able to have a proper classification of the financing methods, and in so doing the authorities may be better able to monitor the financial inflows and outflows in the real estate sector.

Notes

1. Dirie, Nuradin (Somalia Analyst, BBC News). 2012. "Somalia: Far from a Failed State." February 20 (accessed July 27, 2012), http://bbcnews.co.uk.
2. Also known as "qat," "qaad," "gat," "jaad," "tchat," and "miraa."
3. There is evidence that khat cultivation is currently expanding into new areas, such as Embu and Nyeri, outside the traditional growing area of Meru, near Mount Kenya, http://www.new-ag.info/en/developments/devItem.php?a=31.
4. Interviews conducted with farmers in Maua, Kenya, May 26, 2012.
5. Interviews conducted with farmers in Maua, Kenya, May 26, 2012.
6. Omar, Kimenyi, and Maimbo all put the total imports of khat into Somalia between US$110 million and US$300 million. Kimenyi states that the khat trade is fairly lucrative, with a significant proportion of the drug originating in the Kenyan highlands and exported freely to Somalia. He indicates that Kenya exports about US$250 million of khat annually, exceeding tea as one of the country's most lucrative exports, with a majority bound for Somalia. Kimenyi mentions that the Kenya National Agency for the Campaign Against Drug Abuse estimates that Kenya exports about US$300,000 worth of khat to Somalia daily.
7. The information the team obtained from Wilson Airport officials is reinforced by Omar, Kimenyi, and Maimbo in their research and reporting on Somalia including the place of khat in the context of its economy and culture and the amount of money spent on its consumption.
8. 9,000 kilograms per day × 365 days a year.
9. Kaufman, David. 2012. "The World's Most Improbable Property Booms." *Financial Times*, November 16, http://www.ft.com/intl/cms/s/2/160f7b24-29b0-11e2-a5ca-00144feabdc0.html#axzz2KbZDuxSl.

SECTION III

Conclusion

CHAPTER 9

Main Findings and Recommendations for Policy Engagement

There has been much speculation about the destination of ransom money paid to the pirates and their financiers engaged in piracy off the Horn of Africa. The assumptions and perceptions by many in the public and private spheres is that such ransoms are moved around and invested in Somalia and in the region. The assumptions are that some of the proceeds from ransom are invested in legitimate economic activities, while other proceeds are invested in criminal activities including fueling further piracy activities.

This study attempted to assess these assumptions and perceptions. In order to do this in an objective manner, key actors in the region were interviewed, including Somali pirates with first-hand experience and insight into the inner workings of the pirate business model. In addition, data were analyzed, when available, to either confirm or raise questions about the assumptions and perceptions we heard. Given the scarcity of credible data, there was a need to cross-check with multiple sources.

The study calculated that an estimated US$339 million to US$413 million was paid in ransoms between April 2005 and December 2012. The study outlines the financial flows from piracy starting with the nature of the ransom negotiations. The study established that, once the ransom payment has been received, it is distributed to low-level pirates, "the foot soldiers" who are sent out to sea, to carry out the piracy operation; local communities who provide "services" to the pirates; and financiers—those who invest in the pirate activities. The study then laid out the different ways in which the proceeds can be moved within and outside of Somalia, through cross-border cash smuggling, Money or Value Transfer Services (MVTS), trade-based money laundering, and financial wire transfers. Finally, the study looks at how these proceeds are laundered, through investment in other activities and business ventures.

The purpose of this study was to:

- Add to the existing knowledge on piracy activities off the coast of Somalia and, more specifically, the illicit financial flows it generates, with a focus on the structure of the flows and, more importantly, on helping to design appropriate policy responses to address the problem
- Identify the flow of funds through the piracy operational chain through analysis of financial and economic data on how the proceeds of piracy are used and are moved through and out of the region and, finally, the destinations of these proceeds
- Identify the areas of vulnerability within the region with respect to combating dirty money as it relates to the flows of illicit proceeds generated by piracy
- Identify where collective action (particularly at the regional level) would be critical to having a meaningful impact, including identifying opportunities for strategic networking, and possible platforms for regional cooperation to build the capacity of relevant public sector agencies to monitor these financial flows.

Notwithstanding the limitations posed by the availability of factual information, the study has resulted in four key findings:

- First, if the financial flows from the proceeds of piracy are to be effectively monitored, traced, and, ultimately, confiscated, then it is critical that there be more cooperation among the countries in the region in this matter.
- Second, some of the proceeds from piracy represent a threat to the stability and security of Somalia and are recycled into financing criminal activities, including further piracy activities.
- Third, significant proceeds from piracy find their way into the khat trade. The khat business in Kenya, particularly, which is not monitored, is the most vulnerable to this risk.
- Fourth, despite the perception that the real estate boom in parts of the region is fueled by proceeds from piracy, the study found that this is not the case. There are other factors that influence the real estate market, including bank credit to the real estate sector. In general, the data and evidence on the ground were so limited that this perception could not be further substantiated. Further research is necessary to determine the financing methods in the real estate sector.

Despite a temporary decrease in pirate activities off the coast of Somalia, piracy still poses a significant risk to Somalia and the region.

We offer five key recommendations that point stakeholders, including practitioners (on an operational level) and policy makers, toward domains of concrete actions that can be taken to mitigate the risk posed by proceeds from piracy. The recommendations are not intended to be prescriptive but rather are intended to provide orientation on what policy direction to take and in which domains. These actions will contribute to significantly mitigating the risk associated with the financial flows from piracy within the region and beyond.

Main Recommendations

Improve Regional Cooperation and Collaboration

The transnational illicit flows of maritime piracy proceeds are an international problem and thus need an integrated international answer. Actions taken by a few countries separately cannot be sufficient to combat the risks associated with the flows from piracy. Given that all relevant stakeholder countries have already committed to implementing effective Anti-Money Laundering and Combating the Financing of Terrorism (AML/CFT) frameworks, this recommendation seeks to reinforce their international commitments and suggest ways in which the AML/CFT framework can be used to tackle the piracy problem in the region. Countries are strongly encouraged to take into account the risks associated with piracy, and develop appropriate measures commensurate with the risks that are posed.

Therefore, there must be a strong commitment by countries in the region to work together in developing collaborative processes to enable the tracking and disrupting of the illicit financial flow of proceeds from pirates' activities off the Horn of Africa. Frontline states should adopt policies and procedures that encourage cooperation, collaboration, and information sharing among all competent authorities within countries and across the region. These policies should be announced and endorsed at the highest levels of government, such as through a signed memorandum of understanding and the ratification of existing regional treaties and conventions such as the IGAD (Intergovernmental Authority on Development) 2009 Convention on Mutual Legal Assistance. Platforms offered by the East African Community should also be explored. Such processes enable countries to build trust among the competent authorities across the border.

Without trust, states are often hesitant to share financial intelligence data in order to assist in targeting, interdicting, seizing, and ultimately confiscating the proceeds of piracy. Moreover, participation by the countries in the region at relevant international and bilateral meetings such as Financial Action Task Force-style Regional Bodies (FSRBs), the Eastern and Southern African Anti Money Laundering Group (ESAAMLG), the Middle East and Northern Africa Financial Action Task Force (MENAFATF), and the Egmont Group of Financial Intelligence Units, would strengthen mechanisms to exchange financial intelligence. Frontline states should identify the primary and secondary focal points within each competent authority and share these contact details.

The rest of the recommendations presented below cannot be implemented effectively without having achieved a strong implementation of this first recommendation.

Deal with Control of Cross-Border Cash Smuggling

A large part of the ransom money procured by pirates is moved in cash by air, land, or sea. Therefore, improving the capacity of countries in the Horn of Africa to adequately detect, interdict, seize, and ultimately confiscate illegal cross-border cash smuggling is paramount to any strategy aimed at tackling the issue of financial flows linked to piracy and other illicit proceeds. An example is using existing channels and opening new ones to exchange operational intelligence information among the various customs and border authorities for countries in the region. Such exchange of operational intelligence can enable the customs and border authorities to have greater impact in detecting, monitoring, disrupting, and interdicting the illicit transfer of cash across borders.

Another area where action is required is increasing the human, material, and technological capacities of the customs and border officials at the main border entry and exit points including the airports, and land border control posts.

Strengthen Money or Value Transfer Service (MVTS) Providers against Criminal Abuses

Development of an appropriate and proportional oversight framework of Somali MVTS operations in Somalia, and improving cooperation and information sharing with law enforcement agencies in countries where they operate will enable authorities to promote a safe and transparent sector and protect them from abuse. The oversight framework needs to be proportionate to Somalia's situation because overregulation would hinder the critical role MVTS play in Somali society. Discussions between Somali MVTS and the Somali government should serve as a basis to ensure a correct balance is struck in that respect. Such seed work will be paramount to the future development of a proper AML/CFT regulatory and enforcement regime framework for Somalia.

The purpose is neither to criminalize MVTS providers nor to overstate the risk. Shutting down MVTS providers or constraining their operation indiscriminately would have a perverse and negative impact on the way financial flows transit to and from the region. Moreover, it would also affect millions of people relying on remittances. The primary goal is to promote the proportional oversight of Somali MVTS while strengthening their business of facilitating the flow of remittance to and from Somalia. Such a balance will not impede the important goal of expanding access to financial services by a significant segment of the population in Somalia.

Increase Monitoring of Production and Trade in Khat in Kenya and Beyond

The lack of transparency in production and trade in Kenya makes the business susceptible to abuse by criminal networks. Developing an appropriate monitoring mechanism by Kenya would assist the authorities in knowing the financial flows into the khat industry. For example, the framework in Djibouti, Ethiopia, and Somaliland can serve as a benchmark for Kenya. Because the khat trade in Kenya is not monitored, it is an ideal investment for anyone willing to launder or move illegitimate funds unnoticed within the region. Effective monitoring of the khat industry is essential to ensure that pirates do not have the opportunity to buy into and take control of the khat business.

Enhance Data Collection and Monitoring of the Real Estate Sector in Countries in the Region

Better data collection will enable countries in the region to know and understand the various financing methods in the purchase of real estate. It will be critical to have a proper classification of the financing methods and, in so doing, the authorities may be better able to monitor the financial inflows and outflows in the real estate sector.

Such monitoring will enable the authorities and the public to avoid making assumptions that are not backed by accurate estimates of financial flows into the sector, that is, what flows are from the formal financial sector, how much of the flows are from remittances, and how much are from informal sources.

APPENDIX A

Human Trafficking Case Studies

Mayumi Ueno, former Project Officer in Charge of Counter-trafficking at the International Organization for Migration's Programme Support Office in Bossaaso, Puntland State of Somalia, from June 26, 2009, to December 21, 2011, shared two case studies with the team that reveal striking experiences of human trafficking related to piracy. The details of these cases, which are discussed below, were gathered during interviews with victims, and testify to the existence of an organized network trafficking girls for sex to pirates. For their protection, arbitrary initials are used in lieu of their real names.

Case Study 1: A.O.

A.O. reported that she was 22 years old when she was debriefed (although her age could not be verified due to a lack of proper documentation). On her way to Garowe to look for a job, she met a woman named Fatuma who offered her a job opportunity as a maid in Galkayo for US$80 a month. She accepted and was transported to Garowe in the back of a truck. Upon arrival in Garowe, she was taken to a brothel frequented by pirates. A.O. said the customers always talked about how they picked up money in U.S. dollars from the sea, which is how she understood they were pirates.

The brothel was owned by a Somali woman named Mona. A.O. reported that between 30 and 40 women worked at the brothel. However, according to Ms. Ueno, "A.O. was also illiterate and, while the figure of 30 to 40 can seem rather a high number for a 'safe house' in Garowe, one could make an informed guess that at least 20 to 25 women were present." All the girls present were reported to be Somalis of comparable age. They had one to two clients per night and no freedom of movement was permitted. According to A.O., neither she nor her fellow workers received either drugs or alcohol.

After a period of time, one of A.O.'s friends at the brothel took her to another brothel in Eyl. After speaking with A.O., the former officer in charge of A.O.'s debriefing and a former UNODC staff member in Nairobi concluded that it was actually not a brothel A.O. had been taken to but a "residence" where pirates lived when they were not at sea. Other Somali girls were also living in the residence, providing maid services and sexual services to pirates. A.O. eventually became pregnant and gave birth inside the residence. Following the delivery, she got sick and said she was "thrown away" because pirates would find her less attractive after she gave birth. According to the former officer in charge of A.O.'s debriefing, there have been other cases reported in which a female recruiter would release a girl, alone with her baby, after she gave birth. When A.O. ended up on the streets, the community brought her to a local nongovernmental organization, which is how she could eventually be debriefed by the International Organization for Migration.

Case Study 2: N.Y.

N.Y. was a minor from Somaliland. She was born in 1994 and went to secondary school. Her village has an important community of former expatriates who returned. Her dream was to go abroad. One day, she and her friend met a Somali woman, whom they said was a neighbor. Apparently this woman offered them a job in Puntland for US$80 per month and promised that this would allow them to save the money they needed to go to the United Kingdom after nine months. One night, N.Y. and her friend sneaked out of their parents' houses and met the woman at a designated place to get transportation using a "long-distance taxi." They were subsequently brought to Bossaaso to a residence where they served as maids and also provided sexual services. N.Y. reported being in a residence with 4 other girls and 15–16 men in Bossaaso. The men lived in rooms with 4–5 people. A girl was assigned to each room, where she served as a maid and also washed the men's clothing, bathed them, and served their sexual desires. N.Y was rescued by her aunt.

N.Y. had not told her family of her whereabouts. The aunt identified the taxi driver back in N.Y.'s village and asked him to take her to her niece. Arriving in Bossaaso, she negotiated the release of her niece directly with pirates at the residence. There was apparently no financial exchange between the aunt and the pirates.

It is assumed that, because pirates have more money than can be absorbed by the local economy, they are not desperately attached to their proceeds and would rather let a girl go than enter into a fight with a community that does not always accept them.

Reportedly, the recruiter was also working for pirates to provide them with other commodities. That assessment confirms other reports received by the UNODC during interviews in Bossaaso in October 2011, where it was stated that some women transporting khat to pirates were also providing them with other commodities, ranging from toothpaste to weaponry and girls.

APPENDIX B

Khat Business

Figure B.1 Money Flows and the Distribution Network Associated with Khat

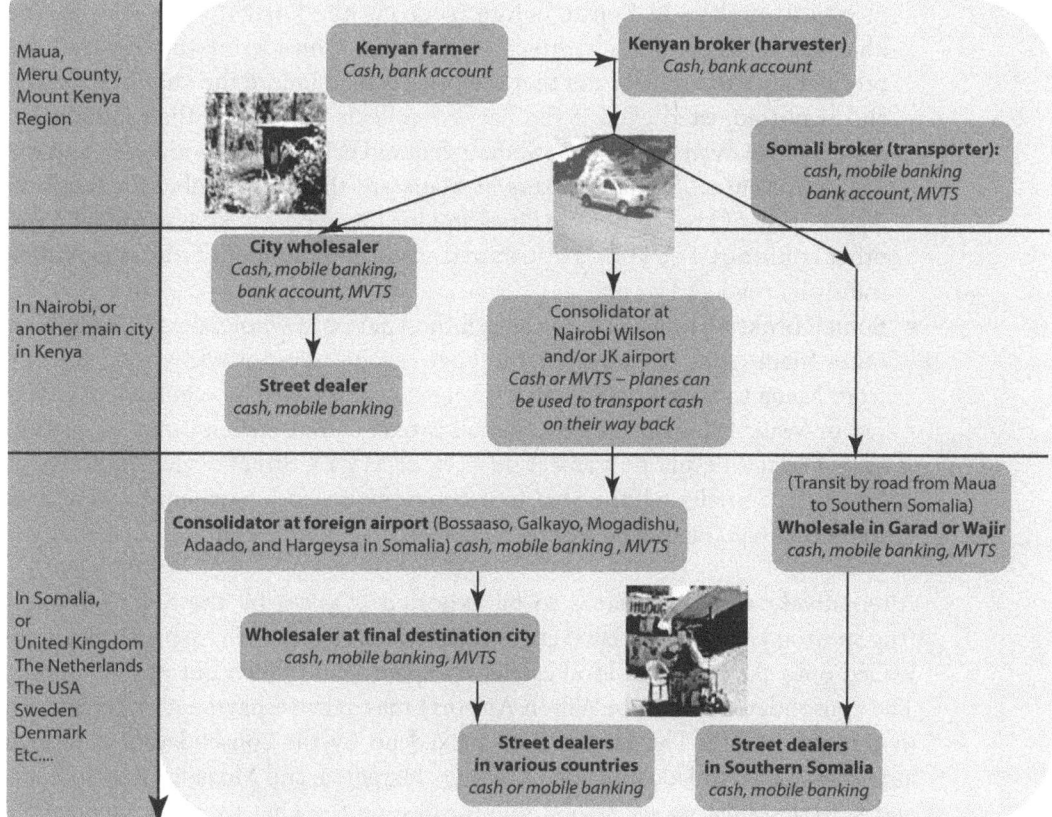

Color code: **Actor involved**
Means used to receive the payment and/or stock and/or move the money around

Source: Formulation based on the team's interviews in Maua.

Based on our analysis, the khat system works as follows:

- The Kenyan farmers are paid in cash for their harvest. They may deposit their money at a local bank office in Maua through money remitters.
- When the khat is ready to be harvested,[1] a negotiation takes place with a Kenyan broker on the assessed value to be harvested by the broker. Once they agree on a price, the broker pays the farmer, harvests the khat, and transports the harvest to the Somali broker. The broker and farmers can be related or can work for the same business entity. The broker is paid in cash or through a Money or Value Transfer Service (MVTS), or may deposit his money in a local bank account.
- The Somali brokers (transporters) are involved from the start of the process in that, based on demands they receive from consolidators and street dealers, they communicate the quantity of khat they need to the Kenyan broker and give the broker the money up front. Consolidators in Somalia also send the money to brokers in Kenya, before receiving the khat.[2] In this respect, the khat market is completely driven by demand. Considering that most of the product goes to Somalia and that the price is paid before the khat is harvested and is not adjusted even if the harvest collects more khat than initially assessed, it can even be said that Somali demand drives both production and the prices in Kenya.[3] Somali brokers in Maua are then responsible for the local distribution of khat to Kenyan cities and for the export of khat to Somalia and other countries. The khat is distributed through a number of routes including transit by road and by air.
- Somali brokers (transporters) can sell the khat onto wholesalers in Nairobi or other main cities in Kenya, or the khat can be transported by road directly from Maua to Southern Somalia, where it is purchased by wholesalers in Garad or Wajir (Somalia). These Somali brokers (transporters) may be paid in cash, via mobile-phone transfer services, or MVTS. Street dealers in Kenya or Southern Somalia sell the khat to users, receiving cash payment by MVTS or as mobile banking payments.

Alternatively, the khat that is to be exported is taken by the Somali brokers (transporters) and consolidated at Nairobi Wilson Airport, where bags of khat are loaded onto the planes of local carrier companies and flown out of the country. The consolidators (Nairobi Wilson Airport) may receive payment either in cash or through MVTS. The khat is then picked up by the consolidators at foreign airports such as Addado, Bossaaso, Galkayo, Hargeysa, and Mogadishu in Somalia, and the consolidators are responsible for passing the khat to wholesalers in the final destination city. Finally, the khat ends up in the hands of street dealers or marketeers in Somalia and other countries including Denmark, the Netherlands, Sweden, the United Kingdom, and the United States, although it is not known exactly how the khat is moved or exported to other countries. The khat is sold to users, and the street dealers receive cash or are paid through mobile banking.

Notes

1. Khat can be harvested about once every four months.
2. Based on interview with pirates.
3. For instance, once a Kenyan broker harvests a shamba at a certain value, if he eventually turns out harvesting more (because the shamba was undervalued), then the Somali broker will not pay the difference but will promise to balance the books over the next order.

APPENDIX C

Real Estate Boom

Djibouti, Ethiopia, and Kenya have all seen increases in property prices, putting them out of reach of a growing middle class. Djibouti has been a magnet for private sector capital investment since 2001, attracting inflows of several hundred millions U.S. dollars, mainly concentrated in the port, tourism, and construction sectors (IMF Article IV Consultation Report 2012, 8–9). In addition, Djibouti has been trying to capitalize on its strategic position in the Horn of Africa and wants to make its port the biggest transshipment hub for the Common Market for Eastern and Southern Africa (COMESA).[1] All this contributes to the high demand for real estate, both residential and commercial. The National Bank of Ethiopia's Annual Report 2010/2011 notes that the investment licenses for the real estate sector grew by 26 percent compared to other major sectors. With respect to the situation in Kenya (the largest and dominant economy in the region), the real estate sector has also grown. Indeed, a 2012 study by a major real estate firm, Knight and Frank, found, for example, that Nairobi was the best performing prime residential market in the world. It found specifically that real estate values in Nairobi grew by a staggering 25 percent in 2011.[2]

Bank Credit to Real Estate Sector

The Djiboutian economy, for example, saw credit to the private sector increase by 23 percent in 2007 owing in part to a real estate and construction boom (IMF Article IV Consultation Report 2012, 8–9).[3] Kenya has also seen an increase in bank credit to the real estate sector. Central Bank of Kenya (CBK) data indicate that the average outstanding loans to the real estate sector over the last seven years has been K Sh 43.1 billion (approx. US$491 million) on an annual basis (CBK Annual Reports 2005–12). Table C.1 compiles the amount of bank credit extended to the Kenyan real estate sector over a seven-year period and provides the average annual credit to the sector.

In addition to the acceleration of credit to the private sector, in Kenya, there is also a large informal economy that fuels the growth of the real estate sector.

Table C.1 Credit to Private Sector (with Focus on Real Estate Sector)

	2006	2007	2008	2009	2010	2011	2012	7-year Average
Credit (K Sh billion)	25.7 (US$293 m)	25.3 (US$288 m)	26.9 (US$307 m)	43.3 (US$494 m)	81.7[a] (US$933 m)	39.5 (US$451 m)	59.3[a] (US$677 m)	43.1 (US$491 m)

Source: World Bank formulation using CBK Annual Reports 2005–12.
a. A review of the 2010 annual report does not explain the sharp rise of credit to the private sector during this period and a subsequent sharp drop in 2011, with another spike in 2012.

The largest of these, situated in the neighborhood of Eastleigh in Nairobi, is a booming commercial center with limited formal control by the authorities. A 2009 study by the Kenyan Revenue Authority found that Eastleigh's informal economy contributed approximately US$13 billion to the national economy—almost a third of Kenya's GDP (US$42 billion).[4] During a visit to the neighborhood, the team saw business booming and intense economic activity, evidenced by skyscrapers, many of which were constructed in the last five years.[5] A Chatham House report puts the Eastleigh economy in the following context, demonstrating its importance to the Kenyan economy and beyond: "Eastleigh is at the centre of a network of trade that connects the Arabian Peninsula, Somalia, Kenya and East and Central Africa, with the Somali business community as the common thread" (Abdulsamed 2011; Manson 2012).

Public and private sector officials pointed to the income generated by the business boom in this neighborhood as another driver of the high property prices and value of the land. In fact, officials interviewed in Kenya indicated that real estate prices have quintupled in the last five or six years, as noted below when discussing the supply and demand for housing in Kenya.[6]

Supply and Demand for Housing

According to a recent World Bank study on the housing market in Kenya (Walley 2011), there is a growing demand for housing driven by a growing population and urbanization. The study found that the housing requirement in 2010 was estimated at 206,000 units, but there were only around 50,000 units being constructed on an annual basis. The shortage in supply of housing units and the increase in demand due to population growth pressures have also resulted in an increase in property prices over the last several years.

Such an imbalance in supply and demand of houses, and greater access to bank credit, will inevitably lead to an increase in real estate price inflation. For example, in Kenya, during the last five to six years, real estate prices have increased 400–500 percent.[7] According to private and public sector players, prices in the Runda, South B and C, and Kilimani areas of Nairobi have grown from 5 million Kenyan Shillings to 25 million Kenyan Shillings (US$58,000 to US$292,000) during this period.[8] A similar observation was made by these interviewees with respect to the Majenga and Nyali areas of Mombasa.

Pirate Trails • http://dx.doi.org/10.1596/978-0-8213-9963-7

Flows of Remittances from the Diaspora

Another key contributor to the real estate growth is the remittances sent to the region by the Ethiopian and Kenyan diaspora. Ethiopia, for example, has seen its share of a real estate boom over the last decade largely driven by government reforms providing incentives to the Ethiopian diaspora who want to buy homes in their homeland.[9]

Ethiopia is one of the few countries in Sub-Saharan Africa that receives large remittances from Ethiopians in the diaspora. According to National Bank of Ethiopia data, private individuals remitted US$2.3 billion in cash and in kind, showing an annual growth of 24.6 percent (National Bank of Ethiopia 2012). Most of this money is invested in the real estate sector. This is consistent with the findings in a 2011 World Bank study on Remittance Markets in Africa. The study found that "most remittances appear to be either consumed or invested in real estate, which offers higher returns than savings deposits and other financial instruments in a high-inflation environment" (Mohapatra and Ratha 2011, 44).

Kenya, like Ethiopia, receives large remittances from its diaspora, which are invested in the real estate sector. The Central Bank of Kenya (Annual Report 2012) notes that remittances to Kenya from outside and within Africa are used for investment, real estate, and education (Kenya IMF Article IV Consultation Report 2012, 11). According to the World Bank, 2009 remittance inflows to Kenya amounted to US$1.7 billion or 5.4 percent of GDP—more than the private sector raised in capital markets for the corresponding period (Mohapatra and Ratha 2011, 155, 157). These inflows are another source of financing that has driven the growth of the real estate sector.

Real Growth in Sector Has Been Modest in Real Terms, Adjusting for Inflation

While it is the case that property prices in a place like Kenya have increased significantly due to supply and demand in housing units over the last several years, a World Bank study on the housing situation in Kenya indicates that the inflation-adjusted rate or real rate of growth is much more modest (Walley 2011, 17). The study found that property prices tripled between 2001 and 2010 at a compounded rate of 12.5 percent. Moreover, the study argues that inflation was running at an average rate of 10.8 percent (using the International Financial Statistics Consumer Price Index Data), which translated into a growth rate for the real estate sector of 1.7 percent.

Notes

1. Interviews of the team with officials in Djibouti in June 2012.
2. http://www.thewealthreport.net/The-Wealth-Report-2012.pdf; http://www.the-wealthreport.net/The-Wealth-Report-2012.pdf, p. 28 (accessed November 18, 2012). The report states that "Price growth in both the Kenyan capital Nairobi and the country's Indian Ocean coastal hotspots outstripped all other *Prime International Residential*

Index (PIRI) locations, with Nairobi property chalking up a 25 percent increase last year. 'Safe haven' isn't necessarily a phrase many people would use to describe the country in a global context, but compared with many of its neighbor's it is just that, according to Ben Woodhams, Managing Director of Knight Frank Kenya. He says that Kenya's rapid economic development is attracting domestic and international private equity, with particular growth in remittances flowing from Kenya's increasingly affluent diaspora."

3. The report states, in part, that a shift has already occurred away from short-term foreign trade financing instruments to the incipient development of a mortgage market, linked to the recent real estate and construction boom.
4. Interview with officials of the Kenya Revenue Authority, May 31, 2012.
5. A visit to the area by the team, May 29, 2012.
6. Interviews with private and public sector officials in Nairobi. Some of the areas most impacted are in Mombasa and Nairobi.
7. Interviews with police, the Kenya Revenue Authority, the Central Bank of Kenya, and a commercial bank in Kenya, May 25–31, 2012.
8. Interviews during the study visit to Kenya, May 25–31, 2012.
9. Interview with the General Manager of Sunshine Real Estate during a study visit to Ethiopia, June 7, 2012.

Glossary

Al-Shabaab. Harakat al-Shabaab al-Mujahideen (HSM), more commonly known as *Al-Shabaab*, is the Somalia-based cell of the militant Islamist group al-Qaeda. The Somali insurgent group Al-Shabaab is NOT listed by the United Nations as a terrorist organization, although several UN Member States have designated it as such, including Australia, Canada, Norway, Sweden, the United Kingdom, and the United States. However, Al-Shabaab is under targeted sanctions from the Security Council Committee pursuant to Resolutions 751 (1992) and 1907 (2009) concerning Somalia and Eritrea. Al-Shabaab pledged obedience to al-Qaeda in February 2012 (BBC 2012).

AML/CFT System. Anti-Money Laundering and Combating the Financing of Terrorism System refers to the legal and institutional measures established to combat money laundering and terrorism financing. See also ML/TF.[1]

Contact Group on Piracy off the Coast of Somalia. The Contact Group on Piracy off the Coast of Somalia (CGPCS) is bringing together all international actors, governmental and nongovernmental, willing to engage in fighting piracy off the coast of Somalia. The CGPCS was established pursuant to the United Nations Security Council 1851 (2008) on January 14, 2009. The CGPCS is divided in five Working Groups, of which:

1. Working Group 1, chaired by the United Kingdom of Great Britain is in charge of naval coordination
2. Working Group 2, chaired by Denmark, is in charge of legal issues
3. Working Group 3, chaired by the Republic of Korea, is in charge of making the liaison between governments and the private sector
4. Working Group 4 is chaired by Egypt and focuses on public campaigns, raising awareness on the problems and danger of piracy
5. Working Group 5 is chaired by Italy and is in charge of tackling the issue of illicit financial flows related to piracy. Established in late 2011 following the 89th plenary session of the CGPCS, it is the last Working Group created.

Criminal control of the economy. For the purpose of this study, criminal control of an economy refers to the control of the economy by actors who are engaged in a criminal enterprise through control of the institutions of government, namely, the executive, the legislative, and the judiciary.

Fragile State. There is no general consensus on the definition of a "fragile state," but broadly, the term denotes a state in which the primary institutions of the state are unable to meet or manage the expectations of its population and capacity through the political process. According to Stefan Wolff (2006), there seems to be a convergence of opinion that the term describes a range of phenomena associated with state weakness and failure, loss of territorial control, low administrative capacity, and political instability.

The World Bank, while recognizing the different criteria used to characterize fragility in a state, considers the term to refer to countries facing particularly severe development challenges such as weak governance, limited administrative capacity, violence, or the legacy of conflict. Most recently, in its *World Development Report of 2011*, the World Bank expands its take on fragility to mean "those periods when states or institutions lack the capacity, accountability, or legitimacy to mediate relations between citizen groups and between citizens and the state, making them vulnerable to violence." For the purpose of this study and in general, Somalia is considered a fragile state.

Financial Flows. For the purpose of this study, financial flows include the money that flows primarily through remitters, cross-border movement, mobile banking, wire transfers, and Money or Value Transfer Services (MVTS); and informal flows through bulk cash smuggling and other illicit (underground) money remitters.

Consider also ***illicit financial flows***, which can be defined as money that is illegally earned, transferred, or utilized through avenues such as commercial tax evasion, aggressive tax avoidance, criminal activities, and corruption.

Financial Sector. The financial sector is the set of institutions (such as money markets, banking institutions, and brokers), instruments and the regulatory framework that permit (monetary and other) transactions to be made.

Khat. Khat (also commonly referenced to as *qat, qaad, gat, jaad, tchat,* and *miraa*) is a small leafy plant. Among communities in the Horn of Africa, the Arabian Peninsula, and in particular in Somalia, the chewing of khat is a social custom dating back many thousands of years. The khat trade in this region is worth hundreds of millions of dollars a year.

Mobile Banking. This is a broad term for the use of a mobile phone to access financial services and trigger a financial event; it does not assume any specific deployment model or any particular transaction type. The term covers mobile payments, mobile transfers, and *m-money*. Mobile banking covers both transaction—and nontransaction—enabling services, such as viewing financial and bank account information on a customer's mobile phone (Chatain et al. 2011). See also Mobile money (m-money).

Money laundering. The process by which proceeds from a criminal activity are disguised to conceal their illicit origins. Most countries subscribe to the legal definition of money laundering as found in the United Nations Convention

Against Illicit Traffic in Narcotic Drugs and Psychotropic Substances (1988) (*Vienna Convention*) and the United Nations Convention Against Transnational Organized Crime (2000) (*Palermo Convention*).[2]

See also *AML/CFT* and *TF*.

Mobile money (m-money) refers to financial services in which customers send and receive monetary value via a mobile phone. This includes retail payments and remittances from one person to another or between businesses. M-money accounts can be provided by many types of institutions including banks and nonbanks, such as mobile network operators and payment system providers. The category of services includes transaction—enabling services, such as domestic or international person-to-person funds transfers or mobile-based payment services. M-money services are part of the retail payment industry and are covered by the national payment system oversight policy. M-money, however, is not a term usually adopted by the community of payment regulators (Chatain et al. 2011).

Money remitters. An activity that involves accepting currency or funds denominated in currency or other value that substitutes for currency from one person and transmission of the currency or funds, or the value of the currency or funds to another location or person, by any means through a financial agency or institution, or an electronic funds transfer network. Often postal service providers fall into this category if they provide fund transfer services.[3]

Money or value transfer services (MVTS). MVTS refer to financial services that involve the acceptance of cash, checks, other monetary instruments or other stores of value and the payment of a corresponding sum in cash or other form to a beneficiary by means of a communication, message, transfer, or through a clearing network to which the MVTS provider belongs. Transactions performed by such services can involve one or more intermediaries and a final payment to a third party, and may include any new payment methods. Sometimes these services have ties to particular geographic regions and are described using a variety of specific items including *hawala*, *hundi*, and *fei-chen*.[4]

Piracy. The definition of piracy used in this study is the same as the one used in Article 101 of the United Nations Convention on the Law of the Sea (UNCLOS) 1982. Under that convention, piracy consists of any of the following acts:

Any illegal acts of violence or detention, or any act of depredation, committed for private ends by the crew or the passengers of a private ship or a private aircraft, and directed:

a. On the high seas, against another ship or aircraft, or against persons or property on board such ship or aircraft
b. Against a ship, aircraft, persons or property in a place outside the jurisdiction of any State

Any act of voluntary participation in the operation of a ship or of an aircraft with knowledge of facts making it a pirate ship or aircraft;

Any act of inciting or of intentionally facilitating an act described in subparagraph (a) or (b).

Pirate. A pirate is a person who is said to have committed any acts that constitute an act of piracy (as defined above). For the purpose of this study, the focus is on "Somali pirates," that is, Somali piracy mainly occurring off the coast of Somalia and the Horn of Africa. The focus of this study is on the "pirate" who is engaged in such acts of piracy off the coast of Somalia and the Horn of Africa.

Pirate Financiers. Pirate Financiers (also referred to as investors in this study) are persons who invest in pirate activities. They are the focus of this study, since they receive the bulk of ransom payments, which are then moved in and out of Somalia and invested into other activities and businesses. Moreover, under UNCLOS, they can be charged with piracy for "inciting or intentionally facilitating illegal acts of violence and detention directed against ship, aircraft, persons or property on the high seas."

Proceeds of Crime. "Proceeds of crime" refers to any property derived from or obtained, directly or indirectly, through the commission of an offense.[5]

Security Council Committee pursuant to resolutions 751 (1992) and 1907 (2009) concerning Somalia and Eritrea. The Committee is in charge of overseeing the implementation of Somalia's sanctions regime, which is regulated by five measures:

The first measure is urging all Member States to "immediately implement a general and complete arms embargo on all deliveries of weapons and military equipment to Somalia until the Council decides otherwise."

The second measure urges all Member States to "take the necessary measures to prevent the direct or indirect supply of weapons, military equipment, technical assistance, training, financial and other assistance, related to military activities, or to the supply of arms, to the individuals or entities designated by the Committee."

The third measure concerns travel bans. It urges All Member States to take the necessary measures to prevent the entry into or transit through their territories of individuals designated by the Committee.

The fourth measure is the freezing of assets. Member States are urged to "freeze without delay funds, other financial assets and economic resources owned or controlled, directly or indirectly, by individuals and entities designated by the Committee."

The fifth and last measure concerning Somalia is the Charcoal Ban, by which Member States are required to "take the necessary measures to prevent the direct or indirect import of charcoal from Somalia, whether or not such charcoal originated in Somalia. Somali authorities shall take the necessary measures to prevent the export of charcoal from Somalia.

In addition, the Committee is in charge of overseeing the implementation of Eritrea's sanctions regime.

The Somali Piracy Business Model. This study analyzes the Somali piracy business model through the criminal networks and the way pirates manage and move their proceeds. These various piracy networks have their own historical developments and are ever evolving "organizations." The study highlights three dominants models of financing an operation and sharing the proceeds—which one could call "business models" for ease of reference, namely the (a) the "artisanal" scheme, (b) the "cooperative" scheme, and (c) the individualistic scheme (Do et al. 2013), all of which are explained in detail in the report.

Terrorist Financing (TF). The financing of terrorist acts and of terrorist and terrorist organizations. The most commonly referenced definition of *terrorist act* is by the UN International Convention for the Suppression of the Financing of Terrorism (1999).[6]

World Bank Report. Refers to a report of the World Bank on the economic aspects of piracy titled, "Pirates of Somalia: Ending the Threat, Rebuilding a Nation." The report shows that it is in the international community's common interest to find a resolution to Somali piracy and help the Government of Somalia rebuild the country. The costs imposed by Somali pirates on the global economy are so high that international mobilization to eradicate piracy off the Horn of Africa not only has global security benefits, but also makes good economic sense.

UNCLOS. United Nations Convention on the Law of the Seas. Entered into force on November 16, 1994.

Notes

1. World Bank, and IMF Reference Guide to Anti-Money Laundering and Combating the Financing of Terrorism, http://siteresources.worldbank.org/EXTAML/Resources/396511-1146581427871/Reference_Guide_AMLCFT_2ndSupplement.pdf/.
2. "The conversion or transfer of property, knowing that such property is derived from any [drug trafficking] offense or offenses or from an act of participation in such offense or offenses, for the purpose of concealing or disguising the illicit origin of the property or of assisting any person who is involved in the commission of such an offense or offenses to evade the legal consequences of his actions; The concealment or disguise of the true nature, source, location, disposition, movement, rights with respect to, or ownership of property, knowing that such property is derived from an offense or offenses or from an act of participation in such an offense or offenses; and The acquisition, possession or use of property, knowing at the time of receipt that such property was derived from an offense or offenses or from an act of participation in such offense … or offenses" (United Nations Convention Against Transnational Organized Crime (2000).
3. FATF definition. http://www.coe.int/t/dghl/monitoring/moneyval/typologies/RepTyp_MSBs_en.pdf.
4. FATF definition.
5. Ibid.

6. A *terrorist act* includes:
   (a) an act which constitutes an offence within the scope of, and as defined in one of the following treaties: (i) Convention for the Suppression of Unlawful Seizure of Aircraft (1970); (ii) Convention for the Suppression of Unlawful Acts against the Safety of Civil Aviation (1971); (iii) Convention on the Prevention and Punishment of Crimes against Internationally Protected Persons, including Diplomatic Agents (1973); (iv) International Convention against the Taking of Hostages (1979); (v) Convention on the Physical Protection of Nuclear Material (1980); (vi) Protocol for the Suppression of Unlawful Acts of Violence at Airports Serving International Civil Aviation, supplementary to the Convention for the Suppression of Unlawful Acts against the Safety of Civil Aviation (1988); (vii) Convention for the Suppression of Unlawful Acts against the Safety of Maritime Navigation (2005); (viii) Protocol for the Suppression of Unlawful Acts against the Safety of Fixed Platforms located on the Continental Shelf (2005); (ix) International Convention for the Suppression of Terrorist Bombings (1997); and (x) International Convention for the Suppression of the Financing of Terrorism (1999).
   (b) any other act intended to cause death or serious bodily injury to a civilian, or to any other person not taking an active part in the hostilities in a situation of armed conflict, when the purpose of such act, by its nature or context, is to intimidate a population, or to compel a government or an international organisation to do or to abstain from doing any act. (UN International Convention for the Suppression of the Financing of Terrorism 1999).

Bibliography

Abdi, Ahmed. 2011. "Puntland Deploys 1200 Soldiers to Ufeyn." *Somalia Report*, July 30.

Abdi, Sahra. 2010. "Mobile Transfers Save Money and Lives in Somalia." *Reuters News*, March (accessed April 4, 2013), http://uk.reuters.com/assets/print?aid=UKTRE62230220100303.

Abdulsamed, Farah. 2011. "Somali Investment in Kenya." Africa Programme, AFP BP 2011/02, March. http://www.chathamhouse.org/sites/default/files/public/Research/Africa/bp0311_abdulsamed.pdf.

Agence France-Presse. 2013. "Notorious Somali pirate 'Big Mouth' retires." January 11 (accessed January 15, 2013), http://www.google.com/hostednews/afp/article/ALeqM5iiEnUeQwm5NFzSihUXdIVvPGX10Q?docId=CNG.ecdbeaab85926ee4b764fabce45ac7b1.331.

Ahmed, Mohamed, and Abdi Sheikh. 2011. "Somali Islamists Want to Do Ransom Deals on Board." *Reuters*, March 1.

AP (Associated Press). 2011. "Somali Pirate Leader Sentenced to Life in U.S Prison." Norfolk, Virginia, December 15.

———. 2012. "Jury to Deliberate Monday on Case of Sex Trafficking." Nashville, Tennessee, April 27 (accessed November 18, 2012), http://www.foxnews.com/us/2012/04/27/jury-to-deliberate-monday-in-sex-trafficking-case986420/.

Ayieko, Francis. 2013. "What Is Financing Kenya's Construction Boom?" *Daily Nation*, January 9, http://www.nation.co.ke/Features/DN2/What-is-financing-Kenyas-construction-boom/-/957860/1661210/-/1v23rx/-/index.html.

Bahadur, Jay. 2011. *The Pirates of Somalia: Inside Their Hidden World*. New York: HarperCollins.

BBC (British Broadcasting Corporation). 2012. "Somalia's Al Shabaab Joins Al Qaeda." Online news article February 10, http://www.bbc.co.uk/news/world-africa-16979440.

BBC News. 2010 "Somali Islamist Insurgents Seize Pirate Haven" (accessed June 1, 2011), http://news.bbc.co.uk/go/pr/fr/-/2/hi/africa/8657060.stm.

Beck, Thorsten, and Munzele Samuel Maimbo, eds. 2013. *Financial Sector Development in Africa Opportunities and Challenges*. Washington, DC: World Bank.

Burgess, Jr., Douglas R. 2006. "Hostis Humani Generi: Piracy, Terrorism and a New International Law." *University of Miami International and Comparative Law Review* 13 (1): 293–340.

Central Bank of Kenya. 2011. "Economic Survey 2010." Central Bank of Kenya Annual Report 2011, Central Bank of Kenya, Nairobi.

———. 2012. "2010–2011 Annual Report." Central Bank of Kenya, Nairobi.

Chatain, Pierre-Laurent, Andrew Zerzan, Wameek Noor, Najah Dannaoui, and Louis de Koker. 2011. *Protecting Mobile Money against Financial Crimes*. Washington, DC: World Bank.

CNN News. 2013. "Somalia's President Wants Partial Amnesty for Boy Pirates" (accessed March 27, 2013), http://www.cnn.com/2013/02/28/world/africa/somalia-boy-pirates-amnesty/index.html.

Davey, Michael. 2010. "A Pirate Looks at the Twenty-First Century: The Legal Status of Pirates in an Age of Sovereign Seas and Human Rights." *Notre Dame Law Review* 85 (3): 1197–230.

Demirguc-Kunt, Asli, and Leora Klapper. 2012. "Measuring Financial Inclusion: The Global Findex Database." World Bank Policy Research Working Paper 6025, World Bank, Washington, DC, April.

Dharoor.com. 2011. "Ali Saleebaan Sub-clan of Majeerteen withdraws its Support and Confidence from Farole Administration." July 27 (accessed July 10, 2012), http://www.dharoor.com/?p=1501; www.dharoor.com.

Dirie, Nuradin (Somalia Analyst, BBC News). 2012. "Somalia: Far from a Failed State." February 20 (accessed July 27, 2012), http://bbcnews.co.uk.

Do, Quy-Toan, Jean-Baptiste Blanc, Aurélien Kruse, Trung Dang Le, Andrei A. Levchenko, Lin Ma, Farley Mesko, Michaela McRee, Claudia Ruiz Ortega, and Anja Shortland. 2013. *The Pirates of Somalia: Ending the Threat, Rebuilding a Nation*. Washington, DC: World Bank.

The Economist. 2008. "Somalia: The World's Most Utterly Failed State." October 2, Nairobi (accessed August 13, 2012), http://www.economist.com/node/12342212.

———. 2012a. "Hung, Drawn and Quartered: Better Deterrents Are Putting the Somali Pirates' Business under Strain" (accessed November 10, 2012), http://www.economist.com/news/international/21565927-better-deterrents-are-putting-somali-pirates-business-under-strain-hung-drawn-and.

FATF (Financial Action Task Force). 2011. "Maritime Piracy and Related Kidnapping for Ransom." Working Group on Typologies, Financial Action Task Force, Paris, July.

Garowe Online. 2012a. "Somalia: Puntland Forces Nab Wanted Pirate in Bossaaso." November 30 (accessed June 26, 2012), http://www.garoweonline.com/artman2/publish/Somalia_27/Somalia_Puntland_forces_nab_wanted_pirate_in_Bossasso.shtml.

———. 2012b. "Puntland Maritime Police Forces Deploy in Strategic Coastal Towns" (accessed June 8, 2012), http://www.garoweonline.com/artman2/publish/Press_Releases_32/Somalia_Puntland_Maritime_Police_Forces_Deploy_in_Strategic_Coastal_Towns.shtml.

———. 2012c. "Somalia Puntland Commando Raid Al Shabaab Operations Base in Golis Mountains." Press Release from the Puntland State of Somali, December 9 (accessed December 9, 2012), http://www.garoweonline.com/artman2/publish/Somalia_27/Somalia_Puntland_Commandos_Raid_Al_Shabaab_Operations_Base_in_Golis_Mountains.shtml.

———. 2012d. "Somalia: President Farole Meets with Clan Leaders in Gardo." March 13. http://www.garoweonline.com/artman2/publish/Somalia_27/Somalia_President_Farole_meets_with_clan_leaders_in_Gardo_printer.shtml.

Geetha, N., and M. Ramesh. 2011. "A Study on People's Preferences in Investment Behaviour." *IJEMR* 1 (6, November), Online—ISSN 2249 (accessed April 4, 2013), http://www.exclusivemba.com/ijemr/App_Themes/Theme1/Images/A%20 Study%20on%20People%20Preferences%20in%20Investment%20Behaviour.pdf.

Greenpeace. 2010 "The Toxic Ships, the Italian Hub, the Mediterranean Area and Africa." Greenpeace Italy Report, June.

Hansen, Stig Jarle. 2012. "The Dynamics of Somali Piracy." *Studies in Conflict & Terrorism* 35 (7–8): 523–30.

Hiterseer, Kris. 2002. *Criminal Finance: The Political Economy of Money Laundering in a Comparative Legal Context.* The Hague/London/New York: Kluwer Law International.

IDA and IFC (International Development Association and International Finance Corporation). 2007. "Interim Strategy Note for Somali for the Period of FY08–09." World Bank, Washington, DC, June 21.

International Chamber of Commerce, International Maritime Bureau. 2011. "Piracy and Armed Robbery Against Ships." Annual Report 1 January 31–December 2010, London.

International Expert Group on Piracy off the Somali Coast. 2008. "Final Report, Assessment and Recommendations." Workshop commissioned by the Special Representative of the Secretary General of the UN to Somalia, Ambassador Ahmedou Ould-Abdallah, Nairobi, November 10–21. INTERPOL. Global Database on Piracy (the use of which is restricted to law enforcement agencies of INTERPOL's Member States).

International Monetary Fund. 2012a. "Djibouti IMF Article IV Consultation Report." International Monetary Fund, Washington, DC (accessed November 21, 2012), http://www.imf.org/external/pubs/ft/scr/2009/cr09216.pdf.

———. 2012b. "Kenya IMF Article IV Consultation Report." International Monetary Fund, Washington, DC, (accessed November 19, 2012), http://www.imf.org/external/pubs/ft/scr/2012/cr1214.pdf .

Jardine Lloyd Thompson Ltd. 2009. *Piracy, Coverage and Response.* London: White Paper.

Jorisch, Avi. 2011. "Today's Pirates Have their Own Stock Exchange; Western Powers Patrol the Seas But Do Little to Stop Pirate Dinancing." *Wall Street Journal* (Online), June 16, http://online.wsj.com/article/SB10001424052702304520804576341223910765818.html.

Kabukuru, Wanjohi. 2012. "Kenya Property Values Among the Best in the World." *African Business*, June 22, Nairobi (accessed April 5, 2013), http://africanbusinessmagazine.com/features/real-estate/kenya-property-values-among-the-best-in-the-world.

Kaufman, David. 2012. "The World's Most Improbable Property Booms." *Financial Times*, November 16, http://www.ft.com/intl/cms/s/2/160f7b24-29b0-11e2-a5ca-00144feabdc0.html#axzz2KbZDuxSl.

Kimenyi, Mwangi S. 2010. "Fractionalized, Armed and Lethal: Why Somalia Matters." Brookings Institution, Washington, DC, February 3 (accessed March 28, 2013), http://www.brookings.edu/research/articles/2010/02/03-somalia-kimenyi.

Maimbo, Munzele Samuel, ed. 2006. "Remittances and Economic Development in Somalia, An Overview." Paper No. 38, World Bank, Washington, DC, November 2006, http://siteresources.worldbank.org/INTCPR/Resources/WP38_web.pdf.

Majid, Nisar. 2010. "Livestock Trade in the Djibouti, Somali and Ethiopian Borderlands." Africa Programme, Chatham House, London, September.

Manson, Katrina. 2012. "Big Money in Little Mogadishu." *Financial Times*, June 29. http://www.ft.com/cms/s/0/d4979b30-bf98-11e1-bb88-00144feabdc0.html#axzz2Cgan4mQI.

McKenzie, David, and Teo Kermeliotis. 2012. "Is Narcotic Khat Funding Terrorism?" March, http://edition.cnn.com/2012/03/07/business/khat-kenya-somalia-al-shabaab/index.html.

Micalessin, Gian. 2009. "Somalia: ostaggi italiani, i pirati si sparano tra loro." *Il Giornale*, April 20 (accessed July 10, 2012), http://www.ilgiornale.it/esteri/somalia_ostaggi_italiani_i_pirati_si_sparano_loro/20-04-2009/articolostampa-id=345073-page=1-comments=1.

Ministry of Planning and Statistics. 2003. "Puntland Facts and Figures 2003." Ministry of Planning and Statistics—Puntland State of Somalia, http://siteresources.worldbank.org/SOMALIAEXTN/Resources/PuntlandFigures.pdf.

Mohapatra, Sanket, and Dilip Ratha, eds. 2011. "Remittance Markets in Africa." World Bank, Washington, DC (accessed November 21, 2012), http://siteresources.worldbank.org/EXTDECPROSPECTS/Resources/476882-1157133580628/RMA_FullReport.pdf.

Mubarak, M. 2011. "Kidnappings in Kenya: Al Shebab's New Direction in Maritime Strategy?" *Strategic Insights* 35 (October): 12.

National Bank of Ethiopia. 2012. "National Bank of Ethiopia Annual Report 2010/2011." Addis Ababa (accessed November 20, 2012), http://www.nbe.gov.et/pdf/annualbulletin/Annual%20Report%202010-2011/Annual%20Report%202010-2011.pdf.

Nenova, Tatiana. 2005. "Anarchy and Invention: How Does Somalia's Private Sector Cope without Government?" Africa Region Findings No. 254, Private Sector and Infrastructure Series, World Bank, Washington, DC, September, https://openknowledge.worldbank.org/handle/10986/9655.

New York Times. 2008. "Somali Pirates Tell Their Side: They Only Want Money" (accessed November 15, 2012), http://www.nytimes.com/2008/10/01/world/africa/01pirates.html.

———. 2012. "Somali Pirates Sent Polite Letters to Ship Owners" (accessed November 28, 2012), http://articles.nydailynews.com/2012-08-15/news/33220721_1_mohammad-saaili-shibin-disorganized-loons-awful-lot-better-chance.

OECD (Organisation for Economic Co-Operation and Development). 2008. "Concepts and Dilemmas of State Building in Fragile Situations." OECD Publishing, Paris.

———. 2011. "2011 Report on International Engagement in Fragile States: Somali Republic." OECD/DAC Discussion Paper, OECD Publishing, Paris.

Omar, Shiine. 2012. "The Khat Conudrum, Somalia's Drug Scourge." January 17, (accessed April 5, 2013), http://www.somaliareport.com/index.php/post/2521.

Opala, Ken. 2009a. "All Roads Lead to Nairobi." Forum for African Investigative Reporters Transnational Investigations, http://fairreporters.files.wordpress.com/2011/11/a-better-life-elsewhere.pdf.

———. 2009b. "All Roads Lead to Nairobi." In *A Better Life Elsewhere, Human Traffic in and from Africa*. FAIR Transnational Investigations, pp. 7–12 (accessed January 27, 2012), http://fairreporters.files.wordpress.com/2011/11/a-better-life-elsewhere.pdf.

Pelton, Robert Young. 2012. "Somalia Report, 'Pirate Leader, Isse Yulux on the Run'" (accessed October 2, 2012), http://www.somaliareport.com/index.php/post/3413.

Rage, Saeed (Minister of Transport, Ports and Counter Piracy of the Puntland Federal State of Somalia). 2012. Address delivered at a conference by the Cypriot Presidency of the European Union on Piracy, Larnaca, Cyprus, November 12–13.

Shawky, Ahmed. 2011. "Worldremit Bids to Transform African Money Transfer." *The Bridge*, September, Hargeisa, Somaliland.

Sheikh, Mohamud Hassan. 2012. "Statement to the UN by the President of the Federal Republic of Somalia." Mogadishu. http://www.soscensa.org/Files/Statement_by_the_president_NY.pdf.

UN (United Nations). 2008. "Report of the Monitoring Group on Somalia pursuant to Security Council Resolution 1811 (2008)." United Nations Security Council (S/2008/769), United Nations, New York.

———. 2010. "Report of the Monitoring Group on Somalia pursuant to Security Council Resolution 1853 (2008)." United Nations Security Council (S/2010/91), United Nations, New York.

———. 2011a. "Report of the Monitoring Group on Somalia and Eritrea pursuant to Security Council Resolution 1916 (2010)." United Nations Security Council (S/2011/433), United Nations, New York.

———. 2011b. "Report of the Secretary-General on the Protection of Somali Natural Resources and Waters Pursuant to Security Council Resolution 1976 (2011)." United Nations Security Council (S/2011/661), United Nations, New York.

———. 2012a. "Report of the Monitoring Group on Somalia and Eritrea pursuant to Security Council Resolution 2002 (2011)." United Nations Security Council (S/2012/544), United Nations, New York.

———. 2012b. "Report of the Chairperson of the African Union Commission on the Implementation of the Mandate of the African Union Mission in Somalia Pursuant to Security Council Resolution 2036 (2012)." United Nations Security Council (S/2012/764), United Nations, New York.

———. 2012c. "Report of the Secretary General Pursuant to Security Council Resolution 2020." United Nations Security Council (S/2012/783), United Nations, New York.

UNDP (United Nations Development Programme). 2012. "Empowering Youth for Peace and Development." Somalia Human Development Report 2012, UNDP, New York. http://www.so.undp.org/shdr/Somalia%20Human%20Development%20Report%202012.pdf.

UNHCR (United Nations High Commission for Refugees). 2013. "2013 UNHCR Country Operations Profile—Somalia." Geneva. http://www.unhcr.org/pages/49e483ad6.html.

UNODC (United Nations Office on Drugs and Crime). 2006. "Coca Cultivation in the Andean Region: Survey of Bolivia, Colombia, and Peru." United Nations, Vienna.

———. 2010a. *The Globalization of Crime*. Vienna: United Nations.

———. 2010b. "UNODC World Drug Report 2010." United Nations Office on Drugs and Crime, Vienna.

———. 2011a. "Study on Illicit Financial Flows Linked to Piracy off the Coast of Somalia." Background document developed for the First UNODC Conference on Illicit Financial Flows Linked to Piracy off the Coast of Somalia, Nairobi, May 17–19, unpublished.

———. 2011b. "UNODC World Drug Report." United Nations Office on Drugs and Crime, United Nations, Vienna.

———. 2011c. Interview with Andrew Mwangura, Director of the East Africa Seafarers' Assistance Programme, Mombasa, October. United Nations, Vienna.

———. 2012. Dataset on pirate financiers.

UNODC-WB (United Nations Office on Drugs and Crime–World Bank). 2012. Dataset on pirate ransoms. (This is a source internal to the World Bank and United Nations and is not available to the public.)

WNN (Women News Network). 2011. "SOMALIA: Human Trafficking Crime Rings Continue to Exploit Women & Girls." WNN Millennium Development Goals Stories, November 17 (accessed July 10, 2012), http://womennewsnetwork.net.

Walley, Simon. 2011. *Developing Kenya's Mortgage Market*. Washington, DC: World Bank.

Wilson Center. 2012. *Drug Trafficking and Organized Crime in the Americas*. Washington, DC: Wilson Center.

Wolff, Stefan. 2006. *State Failure in a Regional Context*. England: University of Bath.

World Bank. 2007. "Global Monitoring Report 2007." World Bank, Washington, DC. http://intranet.worldbank.org/WBSITE/INTRANET/UNITS/DEC/INTGLOBALMONITORING/INTGLOMONREP2007/0,menuPK:3413204~pagePK:64218946~piPK:64218945~theSitePK:3413192,00.html.

———. 2011a. "World Development Report 2011—Conflict, Security and Development." http://siteresources.worldbank.org/INTWDRS/Resources/WDR2011_Full_Text.pdf.

———. 2011b. *Yes Africa Can: Success Stories from a Dynamic Continent*. Washington, DC: World Bank.

———. 2012. "Horn of Africa Situation Report No. 16." August/September, World Bank, Washington, DC.

———. 2013. *Interim Strategy Note for Somalia*. Washington, DC: World Bank.

Environmental Benefits Statement

The World Bank Group is committed to reducing its environmental footprint. In support of this commitment, the Bank's Publishing and Knowledge Division leverages electronic publishing options and print-on-demand technology, which is located in regional hubs worldwide. Together, these initiatives enable print runs to be lowered and shipping distances decreased, resulting in reduced paper consumption, chemical use, greenhouse gas emissions, and waste.

The Publishing and Knowledge Division follows the recommended standards for paper use set by the Green Press Initiative. Whenever possible, books are printed on 50% to 100% postconsumer recycled paper, and at least 50% of the fiber in our book paper is either unbleached or bleached using Totally Chlorine free (TCF), Processed Chlorine Free (PCF), or Enhanced Elemental Chlorine Free (EECF) processes.

More information about the Bank's environmental philosophy can be found at http://crinfo.worldbank.org/wbcrinfo/node/4.